LYNDON
JOHNSON'S
WAR

ALSO BY MICHAEL H. HUNT

Crises in U.S. Foreign Policy:
An International History Reader (1996)

The Genesis of Chinese Communist Foreign Policy (1996)

Toward a History of Chinese Communist Foreign Relations,
1920s–1960s: Personalities and Interpretive Approaches
(co-editor) (1995)

Ideology and U.S. Foreign Policy (1987)

The Making of a Special Relationship:
The United States and China to 1914 (1983)

Frontier Defense and the Open Door:
Manchuria in Chinese-American Relations, 1895–1911 (1973)

LYNDON JOHNSON'S WAR

America's Cold War Crusade in Vietnam,
1945–1968

MICHAEL H. HUNT

A CRITICAL ISSUE

 HILL AND WANG
A division of Farrar, Straus and Giroux   New York

LIBRARY OF CONGRESS CATALOGING-IN-PUBLICATION DATA
Hunt, Michael H.
Lyndon Johnson's war : America's cold war crusade in Vietnam,
1945-1968 : a critical issue / Michael H. Hunt ; consulting editor,
Eric Foner.
    p.   cm.
1. Vietnamese Conflict, 1961-1975—United States.   2. United
States—Foreign relations—Vietnam.   3. Vietnam—Foreign relations—
United States.   4. Vietnam—History—1945-1975.   5. Johnson, Lyndon
B. (Lyndon Baines), 1908-1973.   I. Foner, Eric.   II. Title.
DS558.H85   1996   959.704'3373—dc20   95-26361   CIP

To the memory of Alan J. Perrault
27 May 1943 – 5 November 1966
Georgetown housemate, Vietnam casualty

PREFACE

Historians writing about their own time, especially when it is still shrouded in controversy, have a special obligation to be candid with their readers about their involvement with that past.

I first encountered the real Vietnam in 1962–1963. I spent two summers with my family in Saigon, where my father was serving in the U.S. military mission. I expected to find the Vietnam depicted in *The Ugly American*, by William J. Lederer and Eugene Burdick. As part of the class entering Georgetown University's School of Foreign Service in the autumn of 1961, I had read that popular volume as part of my orientation. I had absorbed its vivid and alarming picture of a communist tide about to wash over Southeast Asia. I had also embraced its notion that Americans with a self-critical, optimistic, can-do spirit—then the hallmark of the Kennedy White House—could save the day.

Once I was in Saigon, my *Ugly American* view of Vietnam found confirmation in the constant press coverage of the struggle against an enemy without a face in a countryside too insecure for me to visit. Then I somehow stumbled on Bernard Fall's *Street Without Joy*. His carefully observed treatment of the travails experienced by the French as they had fought to hold on to Indochina gave me a glimpse of their resourceful and determined enemy, the same one now confronting the Americans. I recall being perplexed that few Americans in Saigon had read Fall's book, and that those who did discounted its insights on the grounds that the United States would succeed where France, a country tainted by colonialism and limited in its resources, had failed.

Doubts stirred by Fall's reportage deepened after I read the third important book in my Vietnam initiation. In 1963, in a steamy Saigon where Buddhists jostled with South Vietnam's government, I picked up Graham Greene's *The Quiet American*. The book's title, which invited comparison with *The Ugly American*, intrigued me. As I read, I was struck by how well Greene knew my Saigon streets, a knowledge he had gained from repeated visits between 1951 and 1955 while watching the Americans displace the French. Having won my confidence, Greene proceeded to unsettle me with his moral vision of those Americans as innocents engaged in a global crusade that allowed little room for national self-doubt or the peculiarities and particularities of the country that they had come to save. And innocence, he observed as though prophesying the horribly destructive war to come, "is like a dumb leper who has lost his bell, wandering the world, meaning no harm."

The conflict in Vietnam continued to haunt me for over a decade. Back at Georgetown I watched with classmates in 1964 and 1965 as Lyndon Johnson moved toward intervention in that country half a world away. Our discussions turned acrimonious. Many of my friends still saw Vietnam in terms right out of *The Ugly American*, while my own doubts about the practicality—not to mention the morality—of waging war had by then deepened. When President Johnson finally committed the country to war, he stirred in me a complicated reaction. I recognized something of my own heritage in the speech patterns, earthy humor, and populist ideals of my fellow Texan. But I also felt an impatience, sometimes difficult to contain, with his sanctimonious invocations of national mission and his mindless repetitions of tired Cold War formulas.

The shadow of the war stayed close during my six years of graduate training in the history of U.S. foreign relations. It clung even closer in 1971 during my short stint at Fort Benning, Georgia, where I went through the basic infantry training for young lieutenants by then no longer needed in Vietnam. As I began teaching, I still felt the war's daily presence in newspapers, television news, casual conversations, and classroom discussions. I longed to open a *New York Times* and not to have to confront the details of bombing in North Vietnam, casualties in the South, or increasingly violent incidents at home. During those years, I was an observer, not an activist—but the convulsion in Vietnam and at home sickened me. I kept thinking of Greene's leper.

The fall of Saigon in April 1975 finally brought peace—of a sort. The war was gone, but not its ghost. While many Americans sought escape, at least at first, in forgetting, my students' questioning shut my door to amnesia. Why had Vietnam happened? Could the war have been avoided or, alternatively, won through more decisive use of military power? What lessons did the war suggest? I briefly wrestled with these questions with a group of Colgate University freshmen in 1978. But I lacked detachment and documentation, the prerequisites for good history. Unequipped for a direct confrontation with the ghost, I backed off and relegated Vietnam to incidental moments in my courses, in my professional reading, and in my private thoughts.

Now, twenty years after the end of the war, I think that the time is right for my own long-delayed exercise in exorcism. When Arthur Wang invited me to do a short history of how we became involved in Vietnam, I accepted. Preparing this little volume on the decision to wage war in Vietnam has served me well. It will also, I hope, address the puzzlement insistently expressed by students and dispel some of the misconceptions still surrounding the war for many Americans, young and old.

Like other great historical events, the Vietnam War offers no easy answers—and no simple moral judgments. If anything, it stands as a cautionary tale to new generations of what the young find hard to grasp—inescapable human limits, the international misunderstanding and miscalculation that inexorably flow from those limits, and the material and spiritual destruction that humans can as a consequence visit upon one another. This is a world, one political wit has pointed out, in which no generation need repeat the mistakes of the past; each is sure to make its own. Such a message may be dispiriting, but an awareness of any people's capacity to play the "dumb leper" may serve as a safeguard against the self-righteous certitude that carried Cold War Americans into Vietnam and that helped open one of the most painful chapters in our nation's history.

ACKNOWLEDGMENTS

I benefited from the first-rate editorial guidance of Arthur Wang throughout this project. A research trip to Texas was made fruitful by Regina Greenwell and the able staff of the Lyndon Baines Johnson Library and by my parents, Phyllis and Wheeler Hunt, who provided a personalized tour of Johnson's Hill Country. Eric Foner, H. R. McMaster, Richard Kohn, and Paula Hunt offered thoughtful criticism of this work in draft. Laura Sell and Chris Endy gave me the benefit of their nonspecialist reading and general assistance. Rachel Bowman, of the Center for Teaching and Learning at the University of North Carolina at Chapel Hill, lent her cartographic skills, while the university's Curriculum in Peace, War and Defense provided financial assistance. To all, my sincere thanks.

CONTENTS

LYNDON
JOHNSON'S
WAR

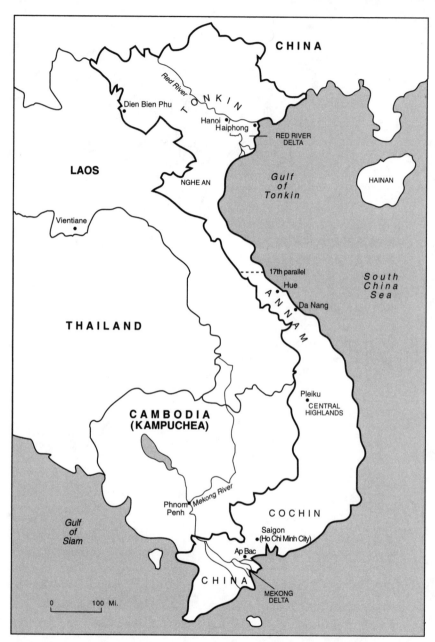

Vietnam

1

—⁘—

THE COLD WAR WORLD OF
THE UGLY AMERICAN

In 1958 *The Ugly American*, a lively, anecdote-filled, and relentless indictment of U.S. failures in Southeast Asia, burst on the American scene. This piece of politically charged, reality-based fiction introduced readers to Vietnam and other parts of Southeast Asia already looming in importance in U.S. foreign policy. Across its pages paraded a small crowd of memorable characters, each with a lesson to teach about why communism* was winning in the region and how Americans needed to respond.

Written in a breezy, accessible style, the book was an instant bestseller. A Book-of-the-Month Club selection, it went through twenty printings between July and November 1958, claimed a place on bestseller lists for seventy-eight weeks, and within its first three years sold two and a half million copies. Americans of all types read the book, including policymakers such as John Kennedy, Richard Nixon, and perhaps even Dwight Eisenhower. The term "ugly American" soon entered everyday parlance to describe ill-behaved, boorish Americans abroad.

This enormously successful book was a collaboration between a recently retired naval officer, William J. Lederer, and a university professor, Eugene Burdick. Through what Burdick called this "message book," they spoke to the faith and fears of a generation whose lives had been deeply marked by the upheaval of World

---

* In this volume, the terms *communism* and *communist* are rendered lowercase when referring to the body of ideas or a proponent of those ideas (as with *democracy* and *democrat*) and uppercase when referring to a particular party or a member of that party (as with *Democratic* or *Democrat*).

War II and the onset of the Cold War. The book's instant and sustained popularity tells much about that generation of Americans, including the leaders who would make the decision to fight in Vietnam and the public that would support them, at least at first.

Lederer and Burdick built their account on a Cold War premise almost universally accepted by their readers—that communism was a dangerous, monolithic enemy whose fundamental values challenged those of the United States and whose ultimate goal was world domination. But what gave Lederer and Burdick's account dramatic tension was not the familiar picture of cynical, cunning, power-hungry communists but the stumbling, ineffectual, and frequently counterproductive effort by Americans on the scene to combat that menace. In sketch after sketch, *The Ugly American* showed how American representatives failed their country. Political appointees, foreign-service careerists, and junketing congressmen all too often lacked cultural sensitivity, command of the local language, a sense of urgency, and an identification with "the people" in the host countries. Perhaps the most memorable of these negative examples was Joe Bing. A diplomat assigned to promote an appreciation of the United States, he failed dismally as a result of his cavalier, almost colonial indifference to local opinion and customs. That he nonetheless moved ahead in his career, while more able colleagues faltered, offered the best testimony to the flaws in the U.S. foreign service.

The authors, however, did not leave their readers without hope. Characters such as Ambassador Gilbert MacWhite, World War II and Korean War veteran Major James (Tex) Wolchek, and idealistic engineer Homer Atkins were the admirable heroes of this influential book. With their notable devotion to duty and their effectiveness at promoting U.S. interests, they helped define an exacting job description for American cold warriors going into the field. To be successful, these warriors for freedom had to be paragons of virtue: tough-minded but humanitarian, friends of the ordinary people yet also able to deal with the elite, advocates of American political ideals but also masters of technology and practical know-how. In the authors' own down-to-earth view, the ideal Americans abroad were salesmen—entrepreneurs of freedom and development—who believed in their product and knew their customers.

The overarching theme of *The Ugly American*, appealing to readers now as much as it did during the Cold War, was that the success of American policy depended in the final analysis on winning hearts and minds. The battles against communism, warned Ambassador MacWhite, would mainly "take place in the minds of men." Or as the authors themselves, writing in a "factual epilogue," put it:

> All over Asia we have found that the basic American ethic is revered and honored and imitated when possible. We must, while helping Asia toward self-sufficiency, show by example that America is still the America of freedom and hope and knowledge of law. If we succeed, we cannot lose the struggle.[1]

. . .

Southeast Asia, the region to which *The Ugly American* so insistently drew attention in 1958, had not been even a blip on the U.S. policy radar two decades earlier. Before 1940, Vietnam in particular was a faraway land, submerged (along with Cambodia and Laos) within France's Indochina holdings, with virtually no record of American involvement and no concrete American presence or interest.

World War II brought Indochina into the picture for the first time. Not long after France fell to German forces, Tokyo extracted from French collaborationist authorities permission to send troops into Indochina. The arrival of the first Japanese units in 1940 suddenly made Indochina a priority for President Franklin D. Roosevelt and his close advisers. Most immediately, Indochina figured as a springboard for control of the region's resources—above all, the oil in the Dutch East Indies needed by Japan's fleet and industry. More generally, Roosevelt realized the region's importance to his prime objective, keeping the British in the war against Germany and the Chinese fighting Japan. Japan's southern thrust imperiled the colonial resources and prestige of his European allies and endangered supply lines to China. With the British and the Dutch able to do little to defend their own colonies, Roosevelt himself sought to deter Japan from taking additional steps south, or—better still—to compel Japan to accept a broad, pan-Asia settlement that would roll back Japanese military expansion.

Once the United States entered the war in December 1941, Indochina receded to a place of peripheral strategic importance. But by 1943, as the Allied coalition glimpsed victory, Indochina reemerged, now as an element in Roosevelt's postwar peace plans. The president himself had made self-determination a wartime rallying cry, to be applied across the board in the making of the peace. He had, moreover, condemned France for mismanagement of its colony. Finally, Roosevelt's distaste for Charles de Gaulle, the leader of the Free French resistance to Hitler's Germany, and for the French people and culture in general reenforced his preference for the decolonization of Indochina.

Roosevelt's anticolonial stand was, however, qualified by a paternalism that was common for his generation and that would prove a consistent strand in later U.S. policy. He doubted the capacity of the peoples of Indochina and other "brown people in the East,"[2] such as the Koreans, to exercise freedom with wisdom. Roosevelt thus concluded that they required a prolonged period of tutelage, casually citing twenty to thirty years as the time needed to imbue them with a sense of responsibility. To ensure a responsible parent for these children, Roosevelt turned to an idea from the League of Nations days, a trusteeship exercised by one or several of the victorious powers. Under this neocolonial arrangement, the peoples of Indochina could gradually move toward their national birthright.

Trusteeship, the device for reconciling self-determination with paternalistic doubts, proved a dead end. Roosevelt could not enlist a suitable trustee. China, nominally a major member of the Allied coalition, was the American president's first choice by virtue of proximity. But China's leader, Chiang Kai-shek, had his own problems at home with his longtime Communist rivals and so demurred. That still left the United States, but Roosevelt anticipated little enthusiasm among Americans for making a long-term commitment to a distant region without traditional ties to the United States.

Roosevelt's British partner in the wartime coalition doomed the already-troubled exercise in decolonization. Prime Minister Winston Churchill had not fought Germany in order to abandon Britain's empire on the whim of the Americans. Not only was he adamant on preserving British colonial claims but he opposed the dismantling of the French empire, which he regarded as the outer defenses to Britain's own vast imperial realm. If Churchill could stop Roosevelt over Indochina, then he could weaken self-determination's threat to his own imperial vision. In this battle for colonial survival, France's leader Charles de Gaulle enlisted enthusiastically. He too regarded overseas possessions as a natural prize for those who fought on the winning side. Indochina in particular stood out as a symbol of French prestige, the repository of valued natural resources, and the home of a privileged and influential community of expatriates. Roosevelt admitted defeat rather than strain Allied wartime cooperation and perhaps even poison postwar cooperation. He made clear only weeks before his death that he was ready to acquiesce to restored French control in exchange for a simple pledge of ultimate independence.

The Indochina issue underwent a dramatic transformation during the five years after Roosevelt's death in April 1945. Cooperation of the wartime Allies gave way to intense Cold War fears. During those pivotal five years, American officials carried forward the paternalism that had been so marked a feature of Roosevelt's thinking. Though few Americans had studied the region or knew it firsthand, officials still harbored deep skepticism about the readiness of Indochina's peoples to govern themselves. At the same time, those officials proved as reluctant as Roosevelt had been to forcefully challenge the French colonial stake there. While they thought that France was not making even the minimum practical political concessions essential to win "native" cooperation and to create the preconditions for independence, they regarded the future of the region as one for the French to resolve for themselves. Postwar U.S. officials thus proved every bit as reluctant as Roosevelt to get involved—at least until the intrusion of global anti-communism as a third, new, extraordinarily potent element in the Indochina mix. The growing conviction that the Cold War was a global struggle provided the catalyst that transformed Indochina into an important strategic area whose loss would have fateful consequences for the region and for U.S. security.

These crosscurrents in U.S. policy were already evident in Harry

Truman's first months in the White House. Roosevelt's successor himself knew virtually nothing about the region and felt no special sympathy for its peoples' demands for independence. Meanwhile, in the State Department, officials based their thinking increasingly on the Europe-first policy of conciliating France. This approach drew support from wartime reports from American observers in China that had described the anti-Japanese resistance in Vietnam (known as the Viet Minh and led by Ho Chi Minh) as a terrorist organization and as a negligible factor in the future of Indochina. Those same reports called for a firm foreign hand, perhaps French, to guide the Vietnamese people toward a nationhood for which they were not yet ready. Americans serving as liaison to the Viet Minh in 1945 offered a notably more sympathetic appraisal of Ho's organization and goals—but to little effect.

When pressed in late June 1945 to take a stance on Indochina's future, the State Department concluded that the independence promoted by Vietnamese resistance groups would produce instability. It also endorsed the resumption of French control. Although it did express hope that France would recognize the need for concessions to the Indochinese and would afford its subjects the opportunity to prepare themselves for eventual self-government, the department discarded the idea of trusteeship and the tattered principle of self-determination and conceded instead outright sovereignty. Consistent with this pronouncedly pro-French policy, the State Department buried deep in its files appeals from Ho Chi Minh to President Truman asking him to honor the wartime promise of self-determination. And the Truman administration watched passively as the French moved to reclaim Indochina, imposing control by force, first in the southern part of politically restive Vietnam and then in the north. By late 1946, Indochina was at war, with the Vietnamese-led Viet Minh spearheading the assault against the French.

By then global anticommunism was beginning to enter the picture. Washington's suspicions of the Soviet Union were gaining focus and force, in turn pushing Indochina toward greater prominence. From his first weeks in office, Truman had countenanced doubts about Soviet intentions that Roosevelt had ignored. By

1946 the Truman administration had privately come to regard the
Soviet Union as a menace and communism as a dangerous doctrine of world conquest. In March 1947 Truman went public in
a major address to the country. He called for the defense of all
free peoples threatened by communist aggression or internal subversion. The Soviet Union had to be stopped wherever it tried to
expand. Climbing on the bandwagon, officials concerned with
building a European alliance against the Red Army were quick to
make the case for Indochina as a critical part of the Cold War.
France deserved support, so they reasoned, as an indispensable
element in building a solid anticommunist bloc in western Europe, the main Cold War front. Thus the French, locked in a
conflict with Ho's forces, and the Americans, in a contest with
the Soviet Union, became different fronts of the same war.

This one-war, many-fronts view encountered resistance from
U.S. diplomats reporting out of Indochina in mid-1947 to a perplexed Secretary of State George Marshall. Despite the risk to
their careers, they questioned the French course in Vietnam and
the French argument that the Soviet Union imperiled the region.
Viewed from their vantage points in Hanoi and Saigon, Ho
seemed a nationalist first and a communist second. He was "the
outstanding representative of the native peoples" and a "symbol
of [the] fight for independence." In practical politics he had
shown himself "a wily opportunist" adept at "straddling the
fence." Although the French tried to help their cause by depicting
Indochina as part of the anticommunist struggle, they in fact had
made a difficult situation worse by driving Ho further to the left
and winning him more popular support. Reverting to Roosevelt's
policy, these American diplomats urged some form of international (perhaps UN) supervision for an Indochina not yet ready
for self-government. Reflecting their own deep-seated paternalism, they feared that premature independence would result in
either chaos or a one-party, totalitarian police state.[3]

Influenced by these on-the-scene assessments, Marshall held
back from embracing the simple equation of Ho with communism
and thus from automatically making Indochina an integral part
of global containment. As late as the summer of 1948, Marshall
was impressed that Ho had advanced his cause with no Soviet

assistance and enjoyed a "large degree of latitude."[4] Practical considerations confirmed Marshall's caution. Resources were scarce, and western Europe and Japan had first claim, far ahead of such peripheral points as Indochina. In any case, throwing good resources into a struggling French enterprise seemed an unwise decision.

In the course of 1949 and early 1950, the Truman administration made the critical decision that Ho was indeed a tool of Moscow—and thus imposed on the region a Cold War logic that led inexorably to U.S. involvement. This decision reflected deepening international tensions. In 1948 the iron curtain had fallen firmly, dividing Europe in two. Then the first successful Soviet nuclear test and the 1949 victory of the Communist Party in China, just to the noith of Indochina, had alarmed policymakers with the vision of a Soviet Union on the offensive. These developments also strengthened the conviction that the French, however self-interested and ineffectual, deserved stronger support as an ally on the containment line.

In February, Washington granted diplomatic recognition to a French-sponsored government for Vietnam headed by former emperor Bao Dai. The secretary of state, now Dean Acheson, explained the step to the president in terms of stopping communism in the most vulnerable part of the region. (He melded into his argument the predictable paternalism by stressing that Vietnam depended on France for guidance to self-government.) Ho was, Acheson announced publicly, "the mortal enemy of native independence in Indochina."[5] At the end of the month, a major report prepared for Truman made a formal case for extending the containment line to Indochina. The report recommended a program of assistance to the embattled French, despite the continuing failure of France to formulate a colonial policy more responsive to "the legitimate nationalist aspirations of the people of Indochina" and more supportive of a Vietnamese government able to rally noncommunist nationalists.

On 24 April Truman finally gave his approval to this report, thus formally and explicitly setting Indochina in a containment framework and at the same time embracing the French as an anticommunist proxy. The United States had made a fateful commitment. The outbreak of the Korean War two months later raised Cold War tensions, the level of funding for Indochina, and the importance of the Asian sector of the containment line. Mounting aid levels reflected the importance now attributed to French Indochina in the global anticommunist battle.

The arguments used in making the 1950 commitment hardened into orthodoxy in 1951 and 1952 and would continue to define official thinking well into the 1960s. At the heart of the orthodoxy was the conviction that communist aggression in Indochina constituted "only one phase of anticipated communist plans to seize all of Southeast Asia." Moscow and Beijing were using the longtime "communist agent" Ho and his "Viet Minh rebellion" to achieve that end.[6] Ho's victory would transform a populous country rich in raw materials into a satellite of the Soviet-dominated bloc. The loss of Vietnam would in turn bring the swift submission of Cambodia, Laos, and other neighboring states of mainland Southeast Asia and set off shock waves that would put at risk U.S. Pacific defenses, Japan, South Asia, the Mideast, and even Europe. In this alarmist intellectual framework, even peripheral losses could cause great damage. In Truman's own words, "To lose these countries to the rulers of the Kremlin would be more than a blow to our military security and our economic life. It would be a terrible defeat for the ideals of freedom—with grave spiritual consequences for men everywhere who share our faith in freedom."[7] So much, it seemed, hung in the balance. Already, in the early 1950s, Vietnam was a nettle hard for American policymakers to grasp, but one that they did not dare ignore.

Dwight Eisenhower came into the White House in January 1953 vowing to liquidate the stalemated and unpopular Korean conflict and to avoid a reprise of limited war on the Asian mainland. While these positions did suggest that the new president would approach Vietnam cautiously, his thinking actually developed along lines virtually indistinguishable from that of the Truman administration. The president and his secretary of state, John Foster Dulles, embraced the commitment to defend Indochina against (in Eisenhower's words) "the implacable and frequently expressed purpose of imperialistic communism to promote world revolution, destroy freedom, and communize the world." The president recalled with special vividness the costs of passivity taught by the recent past (in what came to be known as the Munich analogy): "[W]e failed to halt Hirohito, Mussolini and Hitler by not acting in unity and in time. That marked the beginning of many years of stark tragedy and desperate peril." Eisenhower's own contribution to the constellation of concerns surrounding Vietnam was to give a memorable name—"the 'falling domino' principle"—to the pivotal place the Truman administration had already assigned Vietnam in the scheme of regional defense.[8]

What changed during Eisenhower's eight years in the White House was neither the goal of containment nor the feared consequences of defeat but the means brought to bear on the problem. Eisenhower had inherited the French as the preferred tool of U.S. policy, and he had continued subsidizing their military effort. American taxpayers shelled out $2.6 billion between 1952 and 1954 to sustain the desperate colonial struggle. During those years, the United States carried well over half the war's cost. But, so the thinking went, better to support the French fight than have the United States take up the main burden of the struggle.

The end for the French—and a new beginning for the United States—came in 1954, in the eighth year of the war. In mid-March Ho's forces launched an attack on the French garrison at Dien Bien Phu, in a hilly region of northwest Vietnam near the Laotian border. The French had sought to lure the enemy into a conventional confrontation, but when they got what they wanted, the outcome proved a disaster. The Viet Minh encircled the garrison and gradually choked it off. Washington focused on the practical steps that might prop up the failing French. Eisenhower rejected out of hand sending American troops into another land war in Asia. Some within the administration, including Vice President Richard Nixon, favored using U.S. air and naval support to save the French garrison. Doubting the wisdom of even this minimal effort, the president took no significant action.

In early May the French garrison fell, just as an international conference to end the fighting began in Geneva under British and Soviet sponsorship. Eisenhower sent a dour Dulles to encourage the French to continue their struggle in Indochina in the interest of the "free world." The French were unwilling, however; nor would the British, once so keen on salvaging empire, now join the United States in a last-minute effort to save Indochina. Sapped by two world wars, the Europeans discovered that they had neither the will nor the resources to contest newly restive subjects. Grimly, Eisenhower and Dulles watched the French decamp. Cambodia and Laos gained independence, but the future of Vietnam—that chief battleground of the anti-French struggle— found the powers meeting at Geneva at loggerheads. Finally, on 20 July 1954, they agreed on a compromise that temporarily partitioned Vietnam at the seventeenth parallel, limited the foreign military presence on both sides of the parallel, and scheduled elections to unify the country in 1956. On instructions from Washington, the U.S. delegation in Geneva merely "noted" the conference agreement but would not sign. The French had capitulated, but not the Americans.

Even before the French surrender, Eisenhower had begun a search for fresh means to halt the communist advance. One notion was a regional security arrangement to stand against further Chinese-backed aggression. By September a loose defense organization had taken form under the name Southeast Asia Treaty Organization (SEATO), consisting of the United States, Britain, France, Australia, New Zealand, Thailand, Pakistan, and the Philippines. But it proved a weak reed for Washington because none of its partners shared Washington's alarm over the spread of communism in the region. Eisenhower would have to look elsewhere for a way to carry out his policy. Repeatedly Americans had bemoaned the French failure to lend support to popular anticommunist nationalists who could effectively combat internal subversion. Now Americans had a chance to do it their way with their own handpicked partners in what remained of Vietnam.

Determined to create a new nation in the south, Eisenhower turned to Ngo Dinh Diem, the offspring of a prominent Catholic family with his own distinctly anticommunist and autocratic political stance. Diem's father had worked as an interpreter for French forces subduing his own angry countrymen during the late nineteenth century (including operations in 1895–1896 in Ho Chi

Minh's home region), and received for his reward a post within the French administration. Ngo Dinh Diem himself had entered the bureaucracy, eventually rising to the post of provincial governor but then retiring in 1933 after falling out with the French. During World War II he had flirted with Vietnam's new masters, the Japanese, to no particular effect. His political career had remained stalled after the war. At odds with the Viet Minh no less than with the returning French, Diem had finally gone into exile in 1950.

It was at this point that the American phase of Diem's political career began. He won the backing of politically influential American Catholics such as Senator John Kennedy, Senator Mike Mansfield, and Francis Cardinal Spellman. Then, with his country about to be partitioned at Geneva, Diem raced to Saigon to assume the post of premier under the old French-created government headed by Bao Dai. Eisenhower offered formal, public U.S. backing to Diem in October 1954, and a major program of military and economic support administered by a growing American bureaucracy soon followed. By 1961, total outlays on South Vietnam's defense would hit $7 billion.

By the end of the Eisenhower administration, the surface signs at least indicated that Diem was a gamble that had paid off richly. He promised victory on the cheap, holding at bay the nightmare of direct U.S. combat involvement. He had consolidated his political control with the help of his family and some 800,000 Catholics who had fled south at the time of partition. Pushing Bao Dai aside in an election rigged by his brother, Ngo Dinh Nhu, in October 1955, Diem had created a new state, the Republic of Vietnam, and made himself president with 98.2 percent of the ballots. He had subdued all organized opposition, easing out the last of the French forces, shattering the gangs in Saigon, taming the armies of the religious sects in the countryside, and striking out at the remnants of the anti-French resistance. By the late 1950s, Americans celebrated Diem as a model nation-builder. His face appeared on the cover of *Time* magazine, and his U.S. sponsors congratulated themselves on their insight.

But those who probed beneath the surface saw reason for worry. By the late 1950s, the American embassy was warning that Diem enjoyed little real popular support because of his stiff, aloof political style, his Catholicism (a minority faith introduced by the French), his favoritism toward co-religionists, and his heavy political dependence on his family. He was not, moreover, making effective use of American aid, and he was hobbling his army by keeping it on a leash short enough to forestall a coup attempt. This distinctly political army thus lacked a sharp fighting edge. His land-reform program had bogged down, and the return of landlords and the forced settlement of peasants in government-controlled "agrovilles" in 1959 had helped foster resentment in the countryside. His policy of settling Vietnamese in the Central Highlands alienated the ethnic minorities (Montagnards) living there, thus creating a valuable opening that his Communist rivals would exploit. Lastly, while Diem had seriously disrupted the old Viet Minh resistance network, he had not destroyed it, and by 1959–1960 the surviving activists had begun to rally their forces and rebuild their organizations.

Back in mid-1954, as the United States embarked on its own Vietnam policy unencumbered by the French, Edward G. Lansdale arrived in Vietnam. An outgoing cold warrior bursting with fresh ideas, he was literally the stuff from which fiction would be made. Graham Greene's 1956 novel, The Quiet American, featured a Lansdale-like character, an American crusader who unwittingly sowed devastation in his wake. Two years later Lansdale again assumed fictional form, this time in The Ugly American as the exemplary Air Force Colonel Edwin Barnum Hillandale. A shrewd, idealistic populist, he was pictured helping the leader of the Philippines turn back a leftist insurgency and then moving to press the struggle in mainland Southeast Asia.

Compared to the character in The Ugly American, the life of the real Lansdale was less bizarre and more revealing of the difficulties Americans were encountering in Vietnam. During World War II, Lansdale had left his successful advertising work in San Francisco for the freewheeling world of American intelligence and covert operations. He joined the newly formed U.S. spy operation, the Office of Strategic Services, and for two decades he worked within the shadow of that organization and its successor, the Cen-

tral Intelligence Agency. His Cold War crusade began in the fall
of 1945, when on a mission to the Philippines he identified the
insurgent Huks as communist-inspired terrorists (even though
they had originated to address an interwar agrarian crisis and had
played a notably patriotic role in the wartime anti-Japanese resistance). Later, in 1950, with the Huks threatening Manila, Washington ordered Lansdale back to the Philippines with a small team
of operatives. His task was to bolster Ramon Magsaysay, the new
American political favorite, and to defeat the Huks. Within three
years Lansdale could claim two victories: Magsaysay was elected
president, and the Huks suffered a string of devastating reverses.

This extraordinary success established Lansdale as an authority
on counterinsurgency and as an Asian expert (even though he
never gained fluency in any foreign language). His insights were
much in demand as conflict in the third world increasingly preoccupied the U.S. security bureaucracy. Lansdale's consistent
message was that a hearts-and-minds approach informed by
American goodwill and democratic ideals could overcome any
communist agitation. An American policy that actively promoted
individual rights, dedicated government leadership, a freely operating opposition party, and fair elections would prove in the
long run far more attractive than communism. Conventional warfare alone would not prevail; it would only make matters worse if
the basic longing of people everywhere for freedom and a better
life was neglected. Lansdale kept coming back to these points—
both in Washington and in the field—with the zeal of a mission-
ary certain of the universal applicability of American political values. In promoting these values, he drew on techniques that he
had learned in advertising—get to know your audience (in this
case, the Asian elite that Lansdale saw as his most critical consumers) and promote your product with energy and unwavering
confidence.

In June 1953 Lansdale made his first contact with Vietnam. As
a member of a military advisory group on a six-week tour, he
traveled widely in the war-torn country. A year later, with the
French defeated and partition underway, CIA chief Allen Dulles
ordered him to turn his attention full-time to Vietnam. Lansdale
settled in Saigon and went to work on the familiar task of shoring

up an anticommunist leader, in this case Diem. To bolster the new Diem government, Lansdale launched the familiar repertoire of sabotage, propaganda, tutoring in good government, upgrading the military, and buying off noncommunist dissident forces. But the results were unexpectedly disappointing. Diem proved less responsive to reform than Magsaysay, and Diem's brother Nhu retained a preponderant influence that always troubled Lansdale. By early 1956 Lansdale had become impatient with Diem's failure to become the George Washington of South Vietnam—the founding father of a new, democratic order in that land. In early 1957 Lansdale left Saigon despondent over his inability to make significant headway against the communist threat.

Already by 1958, even as *The Ugly American* commanded a widening readership, Lansdale's own experience challenged the notion that responsible, middle-of-the-road Asian leaders, properly persuaded, would follow the American lead toward democracy and reform essential to blocking the communist advance. The self-righteous presumption of Lansdale and others that Americans had the answers to Vietnam's future and the right to promote those answers was simply a fresh expression of a paternalism that Franklin Roosevelt had passed along to his Cold War successors. As events would prove, this paternalistic faith carried greater risks than anyone guessed at the time. For if freedom-loving Vietnamese did not themselves recognize the severity of the threat confronting them and implement a winning strategy, then Americans would have to step forward and take over the direction of the conflict.

This American paternalism was closely tied to a simple picture of Asians as either easily educable friends or implacable communist foes. In this American view, the friendly Vietnamese were the vast majority of the population—simple, warm-hearted, hard-working people—together with their anticommunist leaders. The "good" Vietnamese instinctively identified with American values and thus were attractive targets for a hearts-and-minds strategy. Honest, dedicated Americans could win their loyalty and guide them away from the pitfalls laid by international communism. On the other side, standing in the way of the U.S. crusade, was a small minority of misguided radicals led by Ho Chi Minh—

those naive Vietnamese who in their impatience for change had fallen into the communist trap. But these deviant natives were in themselves less important than the people who stood behind and manipulated them, the leaders of the Soviet Union and China. Communism in Vietnam was thus seemingly a political movement in thrall to cynical, exploitative foreign powers and out of touch with the real spirit of the people.

Getting beyond these caricatures of the friendly native and his foil, the wily, wild-eyed radical, would have taken a knowledge of Vietnam's peasantry, a sensitivity to its history and culture, and a fluency in its language. Lansdale did not have the necessary tools, and neither did Eisenhower and his immediate entourage. And none of them could acquire these prerequisites to understanding by a few weeks of hurried schooling or by fleeting conversations on a city street or rural lane. Nor could they rely on a hail-fellow-well-met relationship to guide elites who were, in fact, less concerned with advancing American values than with winning the backing of powerful American emissaries with deep pockets.

Had a deeper and more subtle understanding of Vietnam developed, American policymakers might have discovered that the identity of interest between paternalistic Americans and willing Vietnamese pupils did not exist. If they had reached that basic insight, they would have set off a cascade of intellectual dominoes: Vietnam might not be the place to wage the Cold War; the costs of a sustained struggle might prove unimaginably high; and the price of abandoning Vietnam might be far lower than those obsessed with dominoes imagined. There was, in short, a Vietnamese world which Americans, immersed in their own Cold War world, ill understood.

2

———

HO CHI MINH'S BROCADE BAGS

Who was this Ho Chi Minh who alternately baffled and upset American leaders? One acquaintance from the 1920s recalled his "small, spare figure in a white linen suit of European cut, which hung loosely on him, his attentive somewhat sad gaze and the walk of a very tired or sick man."[1] Some of the multitude of aliases that Ho carried tell us something about his outlook and about the nationalist appeal that he would ultimately exercise over many Vietnamese. Perhaps the best-known was Nguyen Ai Quoc (Nguyen the Patriot), but for a time he called himself Nguyen O Phap (Nguyen Who Hates the French) before finally, in 1945, assuming the name by which he would come to be known around the world, Ho Chi Minh (Ho Who Aspires to Enlightenment).

Ho had been born into a highly politicized milieu in the early 1890s (the exact date is disputed). His home province of Nghe An, located in northern Annam, was militantly anti-French. Impatient with royal compromise in the mid-1870s as the foreigners pressed north, Ho's immediate ancestors had joined their neighbors in boasting a readiness to fight with columns of troops "as long as our rivers" and with a courage "as high as our mountains."[2] Ho's father, educated in the Confucian classics, had qualified for service in the bureaucracy but refused to work for a court compromised by repeated capitulation and operating under the thumb of the French. His dissident view seems to have rubbed off on his children. Ho, named by his father at age ten Nguyen Tat Thanh (Nguyen Who Will Be Victorious), joined siblings in clandestine anticolonial activity. Schooled in both Chinese classical and Western studies, he taught for a brief time and then, in 1911, boarded a ship bound for Europe.

In 1917 Ho arrived in a Paris darkened by the clouds of war. He kept body and soul together by using his command of the calligraphy brush to paint antiques or retouch photos, while pursuing independence for his country. He felt a burning resentment over "the crimes committed by the French colonialists in Viet Nam," and sought in the very capital of his country's oppressor some way to end that oppression.[3] Ho cultivated the Vietnamese laborers brought to France to support the war effort, and he established easy rapport with other representatives from colonies seeking justice.

But when Ho turned to seek sympathy from Westerners, he encountered dead ends. U.S. president Woodrow Wilson had loudly pronounced World War I a struggle for a just international order that included national self-determination, and so in 1919 Ho had joined in appealing to the victorious Allied powers for support. He was ignored. Ho then plunged into the debates of the French political left, hoping to find there sympathy for dismantling colonialism. He attended Socialist Party meetings only to emerge doubtful of backing from that quarter. France's own Communist Party, which Ho helped found, fared only marginally better when measured against the essential litmus test: condemning colonialism and siding with downtrodden colonial peoples.

In mid-1920 a copy of Vladimir Lenin's "Theses on the National and Colonial Questions" fell into Ho's hands. Ho would later recall his mounting excitement as he read Lenin's strategy for anticolonial struggle. At first he found in that work

political terms that were difficult to understand. But by reading them again and again finally I was able to grasp the essential part. What emotion, enthusiasm, enlightenment and confidence they communicated to me! I wept for joy. Sitting by myself in my room, I would shout as if I were addressing large crowds: "Dear martyr compatriots! This is what we need, this is our path to liberation!"[4]

Lenin, the leader of the Bolsheviks and founder of the Soviet Union, had passed Ho's test, and Ho responded by embracing the Communist International (Comintern) established by the new Soviet government to carry the revolutionary banner around the globe.

The young Vietnamese had taken a decisive turn down a path that would, three decades later, establish him as Washington's bête noire in Southeast Asia. Ho now drifted into the service of the Comintern. Sometime early in the 1920s, while still in Paris, he began to receive a Comintern subsidy, and then around 1923 made his first pilgrimage to Moscow. By 1924 he was in Canton, the capital of the Chinese Nationalist government, then in alliance with the Soviet Union.

Between 1925 and 1930, still in exile, Ho labored to organize Vietnam's own communist movement. He helped create the Vietnamese Revolutionary Youth League, an important stepping-stone away from political activity guided by loyalty to a particular leader and place and toward a theoretically grounded program that was national in scope. In February 1930, worried about feuding among rival Vietnamese communist groups and prompted by the Comintern, Ho chaired a meeting in Hong Kong to create a unified party. On the Comintern's insistence, the new party was called the Indochinese—rather than the Vietnamese—Communist Party to encourage a coordinated drive against colonialism in the region.

The next decade brought Ho adversity and obscurity. He was imprisoned by British authorities in Hong Kong, but he escaped to Shanghai and thence to Moscow. There he worked for the Comintern during the dark years of the Stalinist purges and distant from the struggling Indochinese Communist Party. Finally, in the winter of 1938, Ho left for China, where he visited Yenan, the center of Mao Zedong's communist movement, and watched for his chance to return home to press the cause of independence.

The onset of global war gave him that chance. In 1940 the German occupation of France and the Japanese occupation of Indochina revealed the vulnerability of the colonial authorities standing in Ho's way. During the winter of 1940–1941, he and his Communist colleagues responded by setting up the Viet Minh (short for the Vietnam Independence League), a united-front organization designed to mobilize a wide range of Vietnamese behind the cause of anti-French and anti-Japanese resistance. As its head, Ho set up a base in south China and made his declared goal not Marxist class struggle but national independence, building on (as Ho put it) "the illustrious example set by our ancestors" and on the support of all Vietnamese: "He who has money will contribute his money, he who has strength will contribute his strength, he who has talent will contribute his talent."[5]

Early in 1941, Ho stepped across the border separating China from Vietnam. His return home brought to a close his period of service as an agent of the Comintern and proved to be an important step toward creating the free, united Vietnam of his dreams. No theoretical giant, Ho would depend on his skills as a master political operator, pulling people together and relentlessly pushing them toward making Vietnam independent. The effort would consume the rest of his life.

The early years back in Vietnam were difficult. The Viet Minh maintained at first only a precarious foothold in northern Vietnam along the Chinese border. Ho himself, while on a mission to China in mid-1942, was thrown into prison by a local warlord. For over a year Ho remained under confinement, whiling away his time composing poems. Some expressed the sardonic humor of a man in chains:

> *The State treats me to its rice, I lodge in its palaces,*
> *its guards take turns escorting me.*
> *Really, the honor is too great. . . .*

Others conveyed his stoic acceptance of this personal setback:

> *The rice-grain suffers under the pestle;*
> *yet admire its whiteness when the ordeal is over.*
> *It is the same with human beings in our time—*
> *to be a man, you must endure the pestle of misfortune.*[6]

Finally freed, Ho returned to Vietnam to direct the Viet Minh and its struggle for national independence through a critical period at the end of World War II. Serving by his side were Pham

Van Dong, the son of a courtier, and Vo Nguyen Giap, a history teacher turned military strategist. They built up versatile, mutually supporting mass organizations. They conducted propaganda campaigns to win popular backing. They trained new political cadres. And they formed the first military units (the seeds of a real army). At all times they kept clearly in view the peasants' hunger for land, and in 1944–1945 dramatized their concern with popular welfare by directing relief efforts and seizing grain hoards held by the wealthy during a terrible famine that took at least a million lives. This varied program helped the Viet Minh to make inroads among ethnic minorities in the rugged mountainous regions of the north and then to extend its reach into the more populous lowlands and even the Red River delta in the final months of the war.

In a 1960 recollection of his political conversion in Paris, Ho described the ideas of Lenin as his "brocade bag." This was a term which he drew from a well-known Chinese tale widely read in Vietnam in which not one but three such bags figured as repositories of ingenious solutions to daunting problems confronting their owner. Ho did indeed draw from one bag the ideas of Lenin as he moved during World War II toward his showdown with the French, and those ideas would remain critical as he later came to confront the Americans. Still Ho had at his disposal two other brocade bags that are also important to understanding the tenacity and ultimate success of the struggle that he would wage.

Perhaps the most important of Ho's brocade bags was not the Leninist one, which Ho had acquired as a young man, but the one containing patriotism, which was his birthright as a member of a small, influential class of well-educated, politically engaged Vietnamese. That class, shaped by the ideal of service to the imperial Vietnamese state and trained on the Confucian classics, was gripped by a patriotic mythology that long predated the arrival of the French. Patriots saw themselves as the carriers of an identity forged over a period of two thousand years of struggle against the pretensions of China, its northern neighbor, and embodied in generation after generation of self-sacrificing commoners and resolute, heroic leaders.

A small country caught in the orbit of a mighty empire, Vietnam had more or less willingly submitted politically to Chinese overlords for its first twelve hundred years, while Chinese ways penetrated and transformed but did not eradicate Vietnam's distinct language and culture. Finally, in the tenth century, the Vietnamese resolved to go their own way, a decision repeatedly challenged by China's rulers. Thus, the Vietnamese had to drive back the Mongols in the thirteenth century, expel the Ming dynasty after a brief occupation in the fifteenth century, and turn back the Manchus in the late eighteenth century. Vietnam was by then poised to reach its imperial apex under its own Nguyen dynasty. A unified country extended its control southward to include virtually all of modern-day Vietnam—only to confront a new, unprecedentedly powerful invader not pushing down from the north but this time arriving from the sea.

The French annexed the southernmost part of the country, which included Saigon and the Mekong delta (Cochin China), between 1862 and 1867, and by 1884–1885 had secured a protectorate over Hanoi and the Red River delta in the north (Tonkin) and the central region (Annam), which included the imperial capital of Hue. Although the imperial court was given to temporizing in the face of French demands, many Vietnamese did not bow quietly. Resistance forces, reported one French observer with a mixture of consternation and amazement, "appear from nowhere, they arrive in large numbers, they destroy everything, and then they disappear into nowhere."[7]

When virtually all armed, organized resistance came to an end in the mid-1890s, the Vietnamese elite found itself divided. While some (including Ngo Dinh Diem's family) continued to serve a monarchy that had become an instrument of colonial administration, others saw themselves as the descendants of patriots who had fought and died for independence and vowed to drive out the foreigners and redeem their country. The latter had been schooled in a national literature of struggle and sacrifice. Those who came to political consciousness in the first half of this century still read Prince Tran Hung Dao's stirring thirteenth-century call to arms against the Mongols. They still knew the proper lessons drawn by the fifteenth-century historian from what was already then a long history of struggle: in quiet days, "teach loyalty and respect for elders, so the people will clearly know their duty toward superiors and be willing to die for their leaders"; and in days of dangers, "man the walls and fight the battles, vowing to resist until death and to die with the fatherland." They still mourned the peasants, who only recently had given their lives in furious, one-sided resistance against the French. They indoctrinated their children, singing them to sleep with patriotic lullabies:

What do we love more than our country?
Our ancestors left us a pot of gold,
Which are the vast four fronts of mountain and rivers.
How many kings have opened up and built this country?
Throughout the four thousand years of stormy weather
How much labor of those who have gone
Is now seen in each foot of river, each inch of mountain, each
*   melon's pith, and each silkworm's innards?*

Little wonder that they would respond to the call to take their place in the long line of dedicated and self-sacrificing patriots.[8]

Leninism, added to Ho's collection of tricks in 1920, provided a way to harness this deep if diffuse patriotic energy latent within the Vietnamese elite. French conquest had discredited the imperial state and left that elite demoralized and uncertain in which political direction to turn. Some considered a reformed monarchy based on the Japanese model; others looked to the established, liberal political systems of the West; yet others embraced radical notions of anarchism and feminism in the intellectual ferment in the 1920s. But a growing number of disaffected Vietnamese were drawn to the Soviet Union. They were especially taken by the Soviet party model—tightly organized, centralized, and disciplined. A party constructed along those lines, with its own ideology and program of action, promised to provide focus and direction to a formidable task—restoring indigenous political authority against a well-entrenched colonial power and then reshaping Vietnam so that it could not only survive but prosper in the modern world. The Leninist party had the additional virtue of promising its adherents that history was on their side and that they would not struggle alone. They would belong to a global fraternity with a shared commitment to a new order. This assurance of sympathy from progressive peoples around the world and especially support from Moscow, in the form of subsidies, training, and refuge, would make easier the difficult struggle ahead.

Party success would in large measure depend on its command of a dedicated, politically conscious body of professional revolutionaries. They were to emerge from a pool of educated youth—for the most part located in cities and working as teachers, journalists, clerks, or students—that had already by the mid-1920s, less than a decade after the Bolsheviks had seized power in Russia, begun gravitating to the Soviet party model. Following its establishment in 1930, the Indochinese Communist Party set about recruiting and training cadres, who constituted the backbone of Vietnam's Leninist party. They served in a hierarchy of cells and committees, extending from the popular base all the way up through successive layers (including notably regional committees) to a central committee and smaller decision-making groups within it, such as the Political Bureau.

The Indochinese Communist Party struggled in its early years. Stalin pushed it along with the rest of the world communist movement toward an emphasis on class conflict rather than national liberation, and the Comintern itself exercised close supervision of party affairs. Moreover, French repression against Communists operating within Vietnam remained severe. In 1931 and 1932 the party was ravaged at every level by a round of arrests, imprisonments, and executions after backing peasant revolts in Ho's home province of Nghe An as well as in adjoining Ha Tinh. Again in 1939–1940, after a period of political relaxation, French police subjected the Communists to a second round of repression. In these years prisons became home, recruitment center, and school for some of the party's major figures.

The third brocade bag contained a populist program. This populist program, which along with Leninism and patriotism filled out Ho's collection, aimed at drawing the widest range possible of Vietnamese into the resistance. It was clear that elite conspiracies against the French were doomed. They were easily monitored by a vigilant secret police and easily smashed. Therefore, a mass base was essential to putting resistance on a sustainable basis and to giving it the collective power to wear down the French.

The notion of building a mass base was inherent in the Leninist party model that the Vietnamese resistance had taken over. It did, however, require an adjustment to take into account the composition of Vietnam's population, four-fifths peasant and short on a proletariat in any sense that Karl Marx would have recognized. To classically trained Marxists, peasants were politically passive and economically backward, and the countryside stood for feudal social conditions. A rural population could not possibly sustain a historically progressive political movement. Marxist orthodoxy instead identified the proletariat as the spearhead for change and industrial, modern urban centers as the proper locus of revolutionary activity.

From the start, Vietnamese Communists made the peasantry an important target of mobilization. They were guided by a mix of practical experience and political necessity. They knew all too well that Vietnam's cities were not only short on workers but also inhospitable and dangerous, a world easily controlled by the secret police. Thus, they adjusted Marx by an easy linguistic sleight of hand. They placed peasants along with workers under the rubric of "propertyless class," the term used to translate proletariat into Vietnamese. With little if any land and shackled by debt, peasants certainly qualified as propertyless.

This determination to reach all "the people" had been evident from the start of Communist organizing activities in the late 1920s. The Youth League cultivated support in plantations and villages as well as factories and mines. Subsequently, the newly founded Indochinese Communist Party rushed to exploit the hardship and unrest created by the Great Depression. Two years of agitation in city and countryside bore the most dramatic results in Nghe An–Ha Tinh, racked by extensive and prolonged unrest following poor harvests. While the Nghe-Tinh violence was unusual in its range and intensity, effectively eliminating French authority for a time, it also served to underline the depth of anger welling up among desperate, hungry peasants and to reveal the vulnerability of rural resistance unless backed by an effective political and military organization. Late in the summer of 1931, French troops and planes finally beat the peasants into submission with heavy loss of life.

These years of organizing and agitating had given party activists an invaluable education. They had learned that the most palpable, pressing enemy of the peasantry was not the foreign occupation that preoccupied the elite but the oppression and poverty of everyday life. They had also learned the wide variety of ills that afflicted peasants, varying from region to region, and everywhere intensified by colonial policy. Peasants had suffered from the erosion of communal land and the outright expropriation of land holdings by colonial fiat (even as population increased in the late nineteenth and early twentieth centuries). They suffered under corrupt and self-serving local authorities aligned with the colonial regime and a legal system skewed against the poor. They faced heavy, fixed taxes and were hurt by the imposition of monopolies profitable to the colonial administration. They were left vulnerable to the swings in the world market as the French pushed local agriculture toward export crops. Finally, village welfare suffered as landlords abandoned their villages for the cities and pursued an impersonal policy designed to maximize returns on their lands.

Communist activists had also learned how they might win support by incorporating into their program fundamental peasant concerns about justice and land. Peasants had shown themselves willing to stand up for their own interests, working through the usual repertoire of protest. They might petition local notables or distant colonial administrators for relief against injustice or hardship, destroy crops and livestock of abusive landlords, and even attack local grain stores, centers of record keeping, and local power-holders and state functionaries (including tax collectors). But these protests tended to be sporadic, localized, and vulnerable to repression, as the Nghe-Tinh rising had demonstrated. It was not enough to win staunch peasant support by redistributing land and ending exploitatively high interest rates on loans and high rents on land. Peasant anger had to be channeled and put on a sustainable basis. Peasants had to be brought into a nationwide organization devoted to defending those gains and offering assurances of a postindependence order that would attend to their welfare.

Equipped with his brocade bags and possessed of a solid foothold in northern Vietnam, Ho would make the most of the sudden Allied triumph in 1945. When in March 1945 the Japanese disarmed and arrested their French collaborators and then, in August, the Pacific War came to an unexpectedly early end, Ho was ready to seize the initiative and make a formal bid for independence. On 19 August Viet Minh forces marched into Hanoi. By the end of the month they also held such other major cities as Haiphong, Hue, Da Nang, and Saigon. On 2 September Ho stood on a balcony overlooking a downtown Hanoi square packed with half a million of his cheering countrymen and proclaimed an end to the French era of misrule and abuse: "A people who have courageously opposed French enslavement for more than eighty years, a people who have resolutely sided with the Allies against the fascists during these last years, such a people must be free, such a people must be independent."[9] Ho's proclamation established a provisional coalition government with Ho himself at its head and laid the basis for the creation of the Democratic Republic of Vietnam (DRV). Bao Dai, the last representative of a monarchy stripped of real power by the French and slowly drained of prestige by its collaboration, had by then abdicated.

The August revolution was a promising bid for full-fledged independence. The Viet Minh commanded the political high ground as the only effective political group in Vietnam with an untarnished patriotic reputation, a national organization, and a demonstrated capacity to mobilize rural support. From that position, it had sponsored a government with national pretensions and broad representation. To strengthen national unity, Ho cultivated a broad range of political groups. Those he could not co-opt, he worked to destroy. To win acceptance of his government within Vietnam as well as abroad, Ho even disbanded, nominally at least, the Communist Party.

From this position of unprecedented domestic strength, Ho hoped to convince the French that colonial control was no longer tenable and that their best chance for preserving a residual stake in Indochina was through a graceful, gradual transfer of full power to the DRV. Even as the war ended, he engaged French representatives in talks, and in the summer of 1946 he transferred the negotiations to Paris, where he sought to reach a compromise. He also appealed to the victorious Allies for backing, on the basis of a presumed common commitment to self-determination. His own declaration of Vietnam's independence ostentatiously opened with a quote from the American declaration's appeal to "life, liberty, and the pursuit of happiness," and then went on to express confidence that the Allies would see the justice in Vietnam's claim to independence. He cultivated Americans serving in Vietnam, and he wrote directly to Washington, hoping that President Harry Truman would prove more responsive to the national aspirations of the Vietnamese people than Wilson had been.

But in fact the DRV's establishment proved the prelude to war. France's colonial residents and administrators proved especially intransigent. Ho returned from his Paris talks empty-handed and with his go-slow policy under criticism from colleagues convinced that a confrontation was unavoidable. Truman was unresponsive to Ho's appeals, and, worse still, the British lined up with the French, helping them get their troops into the British occupation zone in the south. When Chinese Nationalist troops occupying the north returned home in the spring of 1946, French forces and administrators moved north. By December 1946, negotiations with the French had collapsed, and in that month what is known as the first Indochina war began in earnest.

Ho retreated into the countryside, where he would draw on his familiar bag of tricks. Among these, the call to patriotic service remained a staple. As before, Ho celebrated patriotism as "an immensely powerful wave sweeping away all dangers and difficulties and drowning all traitors and aggressors."[10] With his dignified bearing and powerful personal aura, Ho himself was emerging as the charismatic embodiment of that ideal. When he spoke the language of unity and sacrifice, he won fervent partisans to his cause.

Still giving shape and direction to the patriotic ideal was the party organization, which reemerged into the public light in 1951 carrying a new name, the Vietnamese Workers' Party. (Cambodians and Laotians, formerly part of the Vietnamese-dominated Indochinese Communist Party, would now have their own separate organizations.) Its membership had grown dramatically from no more than about five thousand in late 1945 to at least several hundred thousand by 1950, keeping pace with the wider range of tasks imposed by the war and the claims to national control. The party recruited cadres in large numbers to conduct the military struggle. By 1950 the force commanded by Giap had grown to 200,000 regulars, backed by well over a million guerrillas and armed civilians, and was preparing to cross over the next year from exclusively guerrilla operations to conventional military actions against the French. The party recruited cadres to build the political base of support down to the village level. Mass organizations at the grass roots enlisted the support of key groups such as youth, peasants, and women. As the party built up its military and party organization, peasant recruits played an increasingly important leadership role, at least at the lower echelons.

The party's internationalist doctrine and connections continued to give Vietnam's independence struggle a claim on the support of fraternal parties. Although Stalin kept his distance, in 1949 he did give the recently victorious Chinese Communists the green light to support revolutionary movements in Asia. When Ho asked Beijing for help in early 1950, Mao Zedong was quick to do what he called his "glorious internationalist duty."[11] In January China, followed by the USSR and the other socialist-bloc countries, granted the DRV diplomatic recognition, and by August a Chinese military advisory team had arrived to help with training and planning operations. Chinese supplies were soon flowing across the border, with the quantity increasing with the end of China's war in Korea in 1953.

Popular mobilization, especially among the peasantry, remained the third critical element in a winning strategy. The Viet Minh had at the end of World War II established a foundation of support in the Red River delta from which it could conduct a village war against the French. But as the Viet Minh developed a wider reach, it had to adjust its rural program to the different conditions within the country. In the north, where most peasants clung to small plots of land, the party attacked usury, while in the south, where peasants were more often tenants of French and wealthy Vietnamese landlords, the emphasis was on land redistribution. This flexible rural program helped to consolidate the Viet Minh hold in the northern countryside and to bring roughly half of the south under its control.

Those who sided with the Viet Minh in Hung Yen province (located in the Red River delta) have testified to this success. One party activist, Tuan Doanh, recalled that after 1949 the resistance had taken deep root there. Villages provided shelter, served as strongholds able to keep an enemy regiment at bay, offered bases for night raids on enemy outposts, and were visited by Vietnamese collaborating with the French only at the risk of their lives. Doan Van Hoc, a poor and less politically engaged peasant, recalled the same period in terms that were perhaps more typical. In 1945 when the Viet Minh showed up for the first time in his village, "I didn't really know what the Vietminh was. Also, I was scared: I was chary of joining them because I couldn't see what good they would do us." By 1947, Viet Minh performance, not propaganda, had brought him around and into a supporting role in the anti-French struggle: "I did my bit by becoming a village security agent, checking people's papers, tracking down poultry thieves, that kind of thing."[12]

The 1954 victory at Dien Bien Phu—made possible by audacious military planning, strong Chinese support, and heavy sacrifices by ordinary Vietnamese on the battlefield—would cap the Viet Minh drive to evict the French. The French garrison placed in late 1953 athwart the major route from the Red River delta into Laos presented an irresistible target. In a campaign directed by Giap, the Viet Minh enlisted peasants to serve as porters bringing the artillery and supplies across rugged countryside to this remote location. With guns dug into high hills overlooking the French camp, a Viet Minh force of 55,000 launched its attack in mid-March. A rain of artillery first isolated and wounded the garrison, and then a system of trenches squeezed the desperate survivors into submission. The victory in early May could not have been better timed, coming just as the great powers meeting in Geneva were turning to the issue of Indochina.

Pham Van Dong flew to Geneva to claim the victor's spoils— only to find both his Soviet and Chinese allies bent on lessening international tensions, depriving the United States of an excuse for deeper involvement in Vietnam, and cultivating France in order to weaken the western European defense community. Together the USSR and China pressed for a compromise in the form of a temporary partition of Vietnam along the seventeenth parallel. Rival forces—those of the DRV on the one hand and those of the French and of the Bao Dai government allied with the French on the other—were to regroup on either side of that line.

After two years, national elections were supposed to reunite the country and determine who would rule. Pressed by his allies, Ho had to accept these terms, even though they gave him less than the total victory he might have expected after eight years of struggle and the exhaustion of the French. Indeed, the terms were hardly different from what he had offered the French in March 1946—a temporary partition with the DRV in control north of the sixteenth parallel and with unification to be decided by referendum.

Despite the disappointing outcome of the war against France, Ho hoped to travel the remaining stretch of the road to independence in peace. Standing before the Central Committee on 15 July 1954 as the Geneva conference was drawing to a close, he characterized the promised elections as a way of completing the process of national unification without exposing an exhausted people short of food and with a war-ravaged economy to another test of arms. Still he foresaw problems. He recognized that partition would impose hardship on southern compatriots, soon to fall under enemy control, and that they would have to exercise patience and courage for the overall good of the country. Ho's major concern, however, was the United States, which was "becoming our main and direct enemy." Ho feared that the Americans might not only take over from the French but also "expand and internationalize the Indochina war."[13] Ho's response was, for the moment, to offer no provocations that might draw the Americans deeper into the contest, but he left unclear what he would do in case the United States sabotaged national elections and tightened its grip on the south. At least in that case, Ho seemed to suggest, the north would have time to develop economically and prepare organizationally for renewed conflict.

Developments in the south would, in the five years ahead, bear out Ho's fears that he had defeated France only to face a stronger United States. Ngo Dinh Diem, installed with U.S. backing in 1954, helped upset Hanoi's conviction that time was on its side. In short order, Diem consolidated his political position and brushed aside the countrywide elections stipulated by the Geneva accords, all while U.S. aid and advisers arrived in a steady stream to bolster his new government in Saigon. Ho faced a dilemma. He could stay with his cautious, go-slow policy at the price of an indefinite delay in realizing his dream of national reunification, or he could embrace a struggle over the future of south Vietnam certain to impose its own high costs. Ho's colleagues were themselves torn. The signing of the Geneva accords had given rise to some dissatisfaction. That dissatisfaction was subsequently intensified by the collapse of national elections and growing repression in the south. Southern cadres were becoming especially critical of Hanoi's passive policy on reunification. They had dutifully bowed to the requirements of the 1954 agreement. After hiding their weapons, some 130,000 soldiers and civilians had been "regrouped" to the DRV as part of the separation of forces stipulated by the Geneva accords. Anxious to return home to the south, they voiced their complaints over the lack of progress toward unification. Meanwhile, those who had stayed behind after the 1954 partition with instructions to keep a low political profile became even more outspoken. As Diem's repressive policy threatened their very survival, they complained against Hanoi's restrictions on armed resistance. Continued passivity, they warned, might cost Hanoi organizational networks and experienced personnel that would be essential in winning the south. One round of arrests and executions (mid-1954 to early 1956) followed by a second (late 1957 to early 1959) badly depleted their numbers and prompted defections. By 1959 the party could count only five thousand members in the south, and those survivors were losing local support and taking flight to remote areas, out of easy reach of Diem's forces.

Le Duan may have been the strongest, most persistent voice for a more active strategy. Born in central Vietnam the son of a railway worker, Duan had begun his rise to prominence by participating in the war against France. After partition he stayed in the south, where he headed the party's southern branch, and then, in 1957, he moved to Hanoi to become a leading member of the Central Committee. In late 1958 he secretly returned for a tour intended to measure the effects of the pounding the southern organization was taking. He found organizations in some places completely wiped out.

Hanoi began to adjust its policy. A dramatic shift occurred in January 1959, when the leaders of the Workers' Party gave cadres in the south greater latitude to use force to protect themselves and their political activities (though not to wage war against Saigon). The shift culminated in December 1960 with the formation of the National Liberation Front (NLF). This government-in-embryo, pejoratively referred to by its enemies as the Viet Cong —short for Vietnamese Communists—was intended to put the southern opposition to Diem on a sustainable, organized basis with its own administration and army. Once more Ho had turned at a critical moment in the national struggle to a united-front organization. Once more he had formulated goals with broad appeal: to expel the Americans, who had stepped into the shoes of the French, and to overthrow the collaborators, who perpetuated foreign rule and oppressed their countrymen. And once more he sought to keep the Communist role unobtrusive.

The NLF made rapid inroads, quickly attracting 300,000 adherents. They included prominent southern dissidents with no open ties to the Communist cause. Like those who had earlier formed the core of the Viet Minh, they were, in the Vietnamese context, intellectuals by virtue of their advanced education (usually under the French). The bulk were professionals, most commonly teachers but also journalists, pharmacists, architects, lawyers, and engineers. They were to staff the NLF's bureaus and provide an underground presence in the cities right under the enemies' noses. Immediately reenforcing their ranks were 4,500 southern cadres who had gone north after partition and who had by late 1960 returned by boat and by hiking down what would become known as the Ho Chi Minh trail.

In the countryside the party brought its experience to bear on a peasantry already predisposed to embrace its program. One party member active in the south recalled, "The peasants felt that they had spilled their blood to drive the French from the country, while the landlords sided with the French and fought against the peasants."[14] Peasants had watched their hopes for winning land rights evaporate as the new Diem government threw its support behind major landholders. Official corruption and other abuses of power further eroded Diem's base of support. Animosity was even greater in areas where Saigon had tried in 1959 to neutralize the old Viet Minh influence by forcing peasants into government-controlled settlements (agrovilles).

This accumulated anger toward Saigon and nostalgia for the

period of Viet Minh control facilitated the task of NLF activists as they carried out propaganda, built mass organizations, assembled part-time local and full-time regional military forces, collected taxes, and assassinated brutal, corrupt, or worrisomely efficient Saigon officials. But the NLF's trump card was the promise of land. That issue (so the activist quoted above remembered) "scratches the peasants right where they itch."[15] So strong was the hunger for land that propagandists could not even allude to the likelihood of ultimate collectivization of agricultural production (toward which the DRV had already begun to move in the late 1950s with the establishment of cooperatives) for fear of shaking peasant support.

From what we know of Long An, a Mekong delta province strategically located athwart the supply road to Saigon, the NLF's appeal to the peasantry and assault on the government presence had already secured widespread administrative control by the early 1960s. When Saigon's forces, limited to the cities and the main roads, fought back with bombing, military sweeps, and arrests, they further alienated the peasantry. The NLF's success in Long An and elsewhere revealed that Diem was in trouble.

Saigon countered in early 1962 with a "strategic hamlets" program (a revival of the agrovilles) intended to reclaim the countryside by creating fortified settlements, bolstered by government aid and hence impervious to NLF subversion or assault. Within a year that program had, under Ngo Dinh Nhu's direction, supposedly created secure points by bringing eight million peasants under government control. But it suffered from a double handicap. Modeled on a plan that the British had successfully implemented in Malaya, it proved inappropriate to Vietnam. In Malaya, resettlement of the majority Malay population into strongholds had proven effective because the resident Chinese, who led the insurgency and constituted its base of support, were cut off from popular support by ethnic differences. In a Vietnam that was for the most part ethnically homogeneous, such divide-and-rule tactics could not work. Relocated Vietnamese villagers remained vulnerable to the appeal of insurgents who spoke their language and shared their values. The plan was also plagued by bad management and misjudgment. Hastily set up in insurgent strongholds, it deepened the resentment of peasants forced to resettle away from their land and to put their money and labor into this government project. This pacification initiative thus had the perverse effect, especially in the Mekong delta and the area just north of Saigon, of driving peasants deeper into the arms of the government's enemy.

What Hanoi had accomplished in the south through the NLF's sustained organizational work became dramatically apparent on 2 January 1963, when fighting broke out at Ap Bac, located in the Mekong delta about forty miles away from Saigon. This telling battle was set in motion at seven that morning, when "flying banana" helicopters flown by U.S. pilots began transporting Saigon troops to encircle and occupy what appeared to be an NLF command center near this hamlet. Those troops had the backing of regional civil guards and a unit of thirteen armored personnel carriers, making for a total of 1,400 men. They had on call artillery as well as helicopter gunships and fighter-bombers. They expected to find 120 enemy, who would surely run when confronted with overwhelming numbers and arms.

The intelligence was roughly correct on the nature of the enemy force. There were 350 NLF guerrillas (mostly regulars) divided between Ap Bac and an adjoining hamlet. They were armed with grenades as well as captured rifles and machine guns. They had a single mortar but little ammunition and scant experience using it. They had no antitank weapons. In Ap Bac, the focus of the collision to come, their main position was atop a large dike with a commanding view of the flooded fields across which the Saigon troops would have to advance. There the combatants dug deep foxholes, arranged for effective fields of fire, and camouflaged their positions along the dike top. An irrigation ditch behind the dike provided a handy communications trench to evacuate wounded, resupply ammunition, and allow commanders to keep in touch with their men. What was a surprise was that this small, lightly armed force had orders to stand and fight, not skirmish and then retreat. In readiness for the coming battle, the NLF commander on the scene evacuated most of the civilians, about six hundred people in Ap Bac and about the same number in the adjoining hamlet.

The first contact took place at seven-forty-five that morning, as the helicopters disgorged the first troops. Within minutes the NLF forces firing from the dike had disabled three American helicopters, and, despite a hail of bullets and bombs flung at them through the rest of the day, they held their ground. The climax came in the afternoon, when armored personnel carriers advanced on the dike. At a critical moment, just as the armor rose toward the top, a squad leader named Dung jumped from his foxhole and threw his grenade at the top of one of the oncoming metal monsters. Inspired by his example, others in the squad followed suit. Panicked by the concussions all around them, the armored unit hesitated and then fled. Fighting finally died off at dark, and at ten that evening the NLF put into motion their withdrawal plan. By seven the next morning, the regulars had reached the safety of their camps.

That force had made the point the NLF wanted to drive home—they could stand against the armor and helicopters recently introduced into the war by the Americans. The NLF had devised techniques to shoot down aircraft and to immobilize armor, and trained its forces in those techniques. They had, moreover, shown they could survive repeated air strikes, while inflicting heavy losses on the enemy on the ground. In the course of the Ap Bac test, they had downed five helicopters, killed eighty of the Saigon forces, and wounded over one hundred. In addition, they could claim three American deaths and eight wounded. The NLF had paid a price of eighteen killed and thirty-nine wounded.

Ap Bac was no Dien Bien Phu, nor for that matter was it comparable in importance to the 1968 Tet offensive that would shake American political resolve. But for any Americans willing to take notice, the battle bore important lessons as Vietnam began to loom ever larger in U.S. policy. First of all, it suggested that disciplined and well-led NLF units could be more formidable than previously imagined. They could clearly do more than maneuver in secret and attack from ambush. They could fight with a determination and solidarity indispensable to a force with limited resources facing a far better armed enemy.

The battle also confirmed an older truth in Vietnam—that advantages accrue to those with local roots and local support. The regular forces at Ap Bac consisted of young men from peasant families much like those of the people of Ap Bac. They were reenforced by thirty irregulars drawn from the immediate area. They fought in a region long sympathetic to the resistance. Some villagers stayed behind to run messages, distribute food and ammunition, and carry away the wounded. After the battle, those same villagers secretly collected weapons abandoned by the Saigon forces and buried the bodies of three NLF fighters who had been out of reach during the hostilities (including the hero of the day, Dung, killed in the withdrawal).

The battle also revealed a South Vietnamese government force suffering from serious deficiencies, some more easily remedied than others. One was poor security. An informant in military headquarters had tipped off the NLF on the operation directed toward Ap Bac well in advance, and on the morning of the encounter Saigon forces on the march used their radios in the open, confirming the attack and its direction. Saigon's forces also suffered from the low level of commitment associated with mercenaries. They wanted above all else to reach the end of the day unbloodied. Determined to minimize their losses, Saigon's commanders on the scene adamantly resisted American pleas to attack. No less serious was a politicized and divided chain of command, designed to ensure loyalty to Diem and frustrate coup plotters but not to wage a determined, coordinated war. Uncertainty over their superiors' backing and worry over their future prospects brought Diem's commanders, once under fire, close to paralysis.

Perhaps most serious of all, the Saigon units operating against Ap Bac lacked the support of rice-roots political organization, indeed stood for something fundamentally antagonistic to peasant interests. The gulf was evident in the background of the commander of the government's elite armored unit. While his NLF counterpart, a man in his forties, had fought in the south against both the Japanese and the French, this officer in the service of Saigon was the son of a southern landlord who had fought on the other, foreign side—first in the French colonial army, which had trained him, and then with the Americans, as the baton of foreign patronage changed hands in the mid-1950s. Differences in wealth, power, and privilege as well as the stigma of collaboration fell between those who took their stand in the villages and those who sortied out with American backing in defense of the new South Vietnamese state.

Finally, the battle of Ap Bac revealed American advisers straining to take over the war from inept pupils waging a halfhearted campaign against the communist foe. Lieutenant Colonel John Paul Vann was one of those American advisers. He had watched the encounter from the air, raging through much of the day as he tried to goad his Vietnamese counterparts into action, to save the lives of the Americans on the ground, and to redeem what was turning into a major humiliation. He conceded at day's end that the enemy's surprising tenacity had proved them "brave men."[16] But he, no less than his superiors, was carried along by the conviction that they could break the enemy if given a larger role in training and arming their South Vietnamese allies or, if necessary, allowed to assume themselves the main burden of combat.

But what even a relatively knowledgeable adviser like Vann failed to anticipate was the damaging side effects of yet deeper American intervention. The latter would feed the illusion among the Saigon military that ultimately the Americans would save their newly created, artificial state. It would also confirm for supporters of the NLF that the struggle in the south was primarily against a foreign invader and secondarily against the elites recruited to serve as their puppets, just as those same elites had served the French. The Americans would cast themselves unambiguously in the ready-made role of historical villain making a grab for Vietnam's sacred soil. However formidable the Americans were, they were playing into the very strengths that Ho could draw from his brocade bag.

In 1960, at virtually the same time that Ho reminisced about his Paris days and his debt to Lenin, Dwight Eisenhower was discussing with his major foreign-policy advisers the Soviet success in spreading communism around the world. Why, he wondered, were people in the third world generally so receptive to communism? Was it the desperation of the many over "bad living conditions" or the ambition of a few consumed by "the hope of power"? Surveying the masters of the national-security bureaucracy then sitting around him, the president observed almost plaintively, "If we could discover the main inducement or enticement which causes persons to embrace Communism, we could perhaps operate more effectively." When Allen W. Dulles, the head of the CIA, suggested that "nationalism played a part in the growth of Communism," Eisenhower at once rejected the insight: "nationalism was not compatible with Communism since the Communists would always bow to Moscow."[17] No one present took up the challenge of grappling with the even more difficult problem —identifying how peasants might define a better life and what they might sacrifice to achieve it.

Eisenhower's mind, even in its moments of perplexity, had no place for the local knowledge that might erode the sweeping abstractions driving U.S. policy and undermine Washington's superficial, simple conception of the "communist" enemy. Those abstractions left nationalism starkly at odds with communism and could make no sense of politically engaged intellectuals as ready to rally against American as they had against French domination. Yet a Leninist party organization that U.S. leaders decried as a totalitarian instrument controlled by Moscow could in fact serve as an instrument of liberation. Hardly politically immature and slavish devotees of Moscow's false faith, Vietnam's Communist leaders wielded that instrument with the skill critical to making the most of their limited material resources and overcoming powerful enemies as they pursued their dream of creating a fully independent, revitalized, modern Vietnam. Finally, a peasantry whose concerns American leaders claimed intuitively to understand proved in many cases neither passive nor apolitical, neither terrorized nor coerced, but rather ready recruits to what appealed to them as a program of economic justice and social welfare.

American policymakers preoccupied with dominoes and monoliths saw no reason to pay any attention to brocade bags. Thus Eisenhower had difficulty seeing Vietnam as something more than the scene of a simple struggle between slavery and freedom or between a communist monolith and a free world. Presidents John Kennedy and Lyndon Johnson would repeat this stark failure of cultural imagination, and Americans as well as Vietnamese would, as a result, pay dearly.

3

LEARNED ACADEMICS ON
THE POTOMAC

In 1798 an easily ruffled President John Adams denounced in strong and sweeping terms the threat posed by the intellectually cultivated with their pronounced sense of superiority and their pretensions to special insight: "Learned academics, not under the immediate inspection and control of government," Adams firmly declared, "have disorganized the world, and are incompatible with social order."[1] This judgment delivered by the second president of the United States might well have been taken to heart by the thirty-fifth. Instead, John Fitzgerald Kennedy leaned heavily on academic types in shaping his foreign policy, and under him they began the process of making Vietnam an undeclared war, a task they would complete under Lyndon Johnson.

With open irony, the journalist David Halberstam called this group "the best and the brightest" in a popular 1972 account of the U.S. misadventure in Vietnam that Adams would have read as rich confirmation of his own views. Published as the American role in the war was drawing to an inglorious close, *The Best and the Brightest* recalled the time following Kennedy's election when "the best men had been summoned forth from the country . . . , bringing a new, strong, dynamic spirit to our historical role in world affairs. . . . It was heady stuff."[2] As a *New York Times* reporter operating out of Saigon in the early sixties, Halberstam had become an increasingly critical observer of the deepening U.S. involvement directed by these "best men," with their sharp minds and attention to hard facts. After returning home, he watched as they carried their country into a disastrous war—one that (to borrow Adams's phrase) "disorganized the world" and proved "incompatible with social order." Halberstam's was a devastating indictment that has stood the test of time.

The men who responded to Kennedy's call to public service were indeed the best and the brightest—highly educated, successful, and self-confident. With their hunger for information and their well-honed analytic skills, they promised to bring a clarity, efficiency, and direction to policy so notably absent (at least in their view) in the Eisenhower years. As masters of scientific management and analysis, they felt sure that they could make the instruments of American policy work for the benefit of their country and the world.

Once in Washington, the brainy newcomers quickly proved themselves committed cold warriors, with a deep belief in the critical international role played by the United States as the champion of the free world. They viewed Vietnam almost completely within the context of the fight against communism, and they approached the task of "saving" that country prompted by the familiar assumptions embedded in the then-bestselling *The Ugly American*. They championed preparation for limited wars, argued for the efficacy of counterinsurgency, laid out the stages essential to nation-building, and sought to harness imposing U.S. military power to a sophisticated diplomacy of signaling and suasion.

As these American-style establishment intellectuals—men entranced with the possibilities of service to the Cold War state—took up Vietnam as a problem to solve, they in effect put themselves on a collision course with Vietnam's own successful establishment intellectuals, consisting of Ho Chi Minh and his colleagues. The elites on the two sides brought to the looming contest not just distinctly different styles and an astounding disparity in resources but also a striking difference in their knowledge of Vietnam. The Americans, with all their brains, confidence, and resources, were to embark on a struggle for a country they did not even pretend to understand outside the broad goals and presumptions of the Cold War, and in the end their ignorance would prove deadly.

The archetype for the American group, and its member ultimately most influential in Vietnam policy, was Kennedy's secretary of defense, Robert McNamara. Born in 1916, he grew up in Oakland, California, in a comfortable middle-class family whose values inculcated in him a drive to succeed. As a youth, he was disciplined, competitive, achievement-oriented, and emotionally self-contained. At Berkeley, where he got the college education that had eluded both his parents, he majored in economics, won a Phi Beta Kappa key, and was active in student organizations. In 1939 he went on to study at the Harvard Business School. His sterling performance there earned him an invitation to stay and teach. This he did until, responding to the call of wartime service, he transferred his specialty, scientific management, from the classroom to the logistics of waging a global struggle.

After the war McNamara would have happily returned to Harvard had not his wife's bout with polio required money for medical treatment. He was thus lured into the better-paying world of big business. Along with a group of other outsiders known as the whiz kids, he went to work at Ford Motor Company, then in some disarray and in need of the methods of statistical analysis and administrative control that had become his specialty. McNamara proved an unconventional auto executive, fleeing the inbred corporate culture of country clubs and cocktail parties in favor of the intellectual milieu of the nearby university town of Ann Arbor, the joy of poetry, the exhilaration of climbing the Rockies, and the company of his wife. He let his business performance speak for itself, and in November 1960—at virtually the same time Kennedy was winning the White House—McNamara became president of Ford.

The president-elect saw in McNamara, the talented manager, an ideal candidate to run the Pentagon. His name was advanced by several influential contacts, including Robert Lovett, a New York investment banker and respected figure in the foreign-policy establishment on whom Kennedy leaned heavily for advice on recruiting his team. Moreover, investigation revealed that McNamara, while nominally a Republican, had in fact supported Kennedy in the election and was "liberal" on such issues as civil liberties and race relations. After two conversations, Kennedy persuaded a reluctant McNamara to serve on the new team. Mc-

Namara knew little about security issues or the Pentagon, but was sure that he could learn and even surer that he could manage a mammoth military establishment with its multibillion-dollar budget, its 4.5 million employees, its competing fiefdoms, and its sophisticated weapons systems to develop and deploy. With a net worth of about $1.2 million, McNamara could now afford to trade a $410,000 job for one that paid $25,000.

McNamara became the eighth secretary of defense and, at age forty-four, the youngest to hold the office. He assembled a staff heavily weighted in favor of people like himself—Ivy Leaguers with sharp minds and good analytic skills. From the outset, he brought to bear on policy problems the relentless interest in detail and devotion to hard logic that had proven successful in the past. Once solutions emerged, he pursued them with the force and directness of a bulldozer. Not surprisingly, McNamara's intelligence, quickness, and drive made life easier for the president, and won Kennedy's gratitude and respect and, later, Johnson's. Within his first year in office, McNamara was exercising considerable influence—over foreign as well as military policy.

Kennedy's secretary of state, Dean Rusk, also carried credentials that gave him a claim to the status of a whiz kid, albeit one compromised by his poor Southern origins. He was born in 1909 into a close-knit family of Scotch-Irish descent. His father had worked the hard-scrabble, red-clay soil of an isolated north Georgia farm before giving up and moving in 1913 to take an Atlanta post-office job. Dean Rusk attended public schools and then worked his way through Davidson, a small Presbyterian liberal-arts college in North Carolina known as "the poor man's Princeton." Rusk's energy, discipline, and talent won him in 1931 what McNamara had badly wanted but narrowly missed—a prestigious Rhodes scholarship for study at Oxford. That award secured for Rusk advantages that were for some of his future Washington colleagues a birthright—an opportunity for foreign travel, an entrée to elite society, connections with important people who could advance his career, and a comfortable lifestyle.

While studying at Oxford, Rusk witnessed Hitler's rise to power, even living for a time in Germany in the throes of the Nazi takeover. The terrible consequences seared his imagination.

Others of the Kennedy crowd also carried away from those years the lesson that the democracies had to take an early, strong stand against aggression, but perhaps on none was that lesson marked more deeply or indelibly. Rusk's later adamant defense of South Vietnam had its roots in this personal experience and was strongly reenforced by his devotion to the ideal of a just international order.

In 1934 Rusk returned home to teach government and international relations at Mills College in San Francisco. Called to military duty in 1940, Rusk became an instant Asia expert during the war years, part of which he spent in a staff position in India. (While there, he authorized at least one supply drop to an anti-Japanese resistance group headed by an obscure figure named Ho.) After the war Rusk moved into the State Department, where he confirmed his ability as a skillful administrator, helped deal with the aftershock of China's loss to communism and with the equally unexpected, drawn-out Sino-American war in Korea, and in the process won kudos from his superiors, first George Marshall and then Dean Acheson. In 1952 Rusk left Washington to become president of the philanthropic Rockefeller Foundation.

President-elect Kennedy did not know Rusk personally, and in fact considered half a dozen candidates for secretary of state before recommendations from Acheson and Lovett swayed his choice. As it turned out, Rusk would stand on the margin of the whiz-kid crowd. He was no kid; his fifty-two years made him somewhat older than the other Kennedy advisers. He also lacked whiz. Practical policy experience had brought him to a philosophical acceptance of the notion that some problems were not easily solved and to a tolerance for the ponderous pace of the State Department bureaucracy. Temperament also played a role. Rusk was soft-spoken and patient, and in formal meetings seemed deferential, even impassive. (He preferred to reserve his advice for the president's ears alone.) He had no taste for the combativeness—both bureaucratic and intellectual—displayed by the other Kennedy newcomers, and he failed to develop an easy relationship with the president. In short order, Rusk was not so much making foreign policy as reacting to initiatives coming out of the Pentagon and the White House.

Closer to the McNamara mold were two prominent recruits from institutions of higher learning on the banks of Massachusetts's Charles River. When Kennedy selected McGeorge Bundy as his special assistant for national security affairs (in effect, his in-house adviser on foreign policy), he was tapping a man with a pedigree, a strong record as an academic administrator, a quick mind, and a strong competitive urge. Born in 1919, Bundy came as close as any American could to inheriting his position. His mother was from Boston's distinguished Lowell family, and his father, armed with degrees from Yale and Harvard Law, was a successful lawyer and a close associate of Henry L. Stimson, a quintessential establishment figure who had served as Herbert Hoover's secretary of state and Franklin Roosevelt's secretary of war.

Bundy himself had added to his claim to power and influence by getting his ticket punched at the right places. He had gone to Groton, the prep school for the northeast establishment, graduated from Yale, and then moved on to Harvard, where for a time he was one of a group of special graduate students privileged to pursue their own unstructured program of study. He served during World War II as an admiral's aide, and after the war worked in a succession of jobs—for the Marshall Plan, for John Foster Dulles's New York political campaign, and for the Council on Foreign Relations in New York—before returning to Harvard. Though without a doctorate, he taught in the government department there, and in 1953 became the youngest dean of the faculty in the history of the university. Bundy proved an adept manager of a faculty with large and sensitive egos. He got things done, brought intellectual excitement to the campus, and kept McCarthyite government inquisitors away (by expunging any hints of communism on campus). He won plaudits for his performance.

The Bundy to whom Kennedy turned for help was not an accomplished intellectual but rather a superior staff man with excellent connections, skill at reading people and situations, an understanding of the bureaucratic process, and a knack for keeping the paper moving. (His one try for public office—what he understood to be a safe seat on the Boston city council—had ended in defeat.) A moderate Republican, Bundy had hit it off with the young Massachusetts senator, and supported his bid for the presidency. Following the election, Kennedy had considered Bundy to head the State Department but deemed him at forty-one too young for the job. He would instead bring Bundy to the White House. Cool, controlled, laconic, Bundy would serve from his basement office in the west wing as the president's foreign-policy gatekeeper and sounding board. Among his first concerns was staffing not only his own office but also other parts of the foreign-affairs bureaucracy with bright young men from Cambridge and New York who had sterling academic credentials and certifiably "sound" policy views.

Bundy's approach to international affairs was guided by a simple, deeply held, largely unexamined, and untested Cold War faith. For him, communism was a deadly foe, and an American policy of "realism" and "toughness," formulated and implemented by people like himself, was the logical response. American leadership was critical. Bundy had learned from Dean Acheson that "in the final analysis, the United States is the engine of mankind, and the rest of the world the caboose."[3] Helping the president figure out how best to drive that engine in a way that was realistic and tough was what Bundy would devote himself to. Bundy's thinking on Vietnam was limited to the conviction that there, as at other contested points around the world, the United States could not accept defeat.

Walt Whitman Rostow, an economic historian from the Massachusetts Institute of Technology, emphatically agreed. This idea man, intellectually combative and academically accomplished when he enlisted in Kennedy's service in 1961, was born in 1916 in New York, the son of Russian-Jewish immigrants. Rostow's combination of intelligence and drive propelled him through his public schooling in New York, on to Yale, and then off to England with a Rhodes scholarship in hand. During World War II he went into uniform and ended up selecting targets for Allied bombers flying over Europe. After the war he went to teach at MIT, where he labored with his colleagues to apply the social-science theories developed in the library and the classroom to the winning of the Cold War. While publishing extensively, Rostow also consulted frequently in Washington.

Rostow had met Senator Kennedy in the mid-1950s and quickly established his value as an adviser. Energetic, enthusiastic, absolutely confident in his judgments, and disarmingly gracious in his interpersonal relations, Rostow could get his ideas across clearly and economically and in terms that made political sense. He was eager for a place in the new administration. When Rusk resisted giving him a position in the State Department, Kennedy brought Rostow into the White House to serve as Bundy's deputy. Rostow liked to think of himself and Bundy dividing the world between them. While Bundy focused on transatlantic issues, Rostow would claim the third world, in which he had a long-standing interest. Rostow thus made Vietnam his special turf, where he could test his prized social-science propositions.

Kennedy may not have noticed a flaw in this set of foreign-policy advisers—their limited range of experience. Neither McNamara nor Bundy nor Rostow had actually had a hand in making policy before leaping to the top in 1961. Rusk, the exception, had climbed no higher than the second echelon. Moreover, these men who would move their country toward war had themselves no direct experience of combat. Finally, none had had any significant involvement in electoral politics, which might have brought them into touch with the concerns of the people who would ultimately fight and die in Vietnam. Sam Rayburn, the Speaker of the House, responded with cool skepticism after an awed Lyndon Johnson reported to his mentor and fellow Texan about the impressive group Kennedy had assembled: "Well, Lyndon, you may be right and they may be every bit as intelligent as you say, but I'd feel a whole lot better about them if just one of them had run for sheriff once."[4]

The forty-three-year-old Kennedy, inaugurated in January 1961, looked like an easy mark for this collection of bright lights. There was an abundance of reasons for fearing that the president lacked the intellect, experience, and character indispensable to a critical appraisal of the inherited, complex, and deeply troubled Vietnam commitment.

To begin with, John Kennedy had developed both personally and politically as a creature of his wealthy, domineering father.

Joseph Kennedy was the family autocrat, who demanded that his children excel and thereby win the social respect and political standing that Boston's Yankee elite had denied him and others prominent in the Irish community. His firstborn son, Joseph junior, had been the favored repository of those ambitions. But following his death in World War II, the mantle of paternal expectations fell on John. He brought to his struggle to live up to those expectations some social assets—notably charm and a sense of humor that his peers found winning. He was, however, slow to mature, remaining in the eyes of his friends something of a little-boy-lost into the 1950s. One college friend described him as "attractive, witty, and unpurposeful."[5] His was a mediocre mind, neither unusually absorptive nor disciplined nor deep. And he suffered from frail health, most notably a bad back and an increasingly serious adrenal deficiency.

His father's money and connections helped Kennedy make up for what he lacked in direction and intellect. He got into first-class schools, first Choate (a distinguished prep school in Connecticut) and then Harvard, from which he graduated in 1940 with an indifferent academic record. He got the chance to travel to Europe. And he even had ghostwritten for him, published, and promoted in 1940 a slim volume, *Why England Slept*, the success of which helped create the illusion of Kennedy as a person of insight and style. The public relations resources at the command of Joseph senior came into play again soon, converting an embarrassingly negligent loss of the torpedo boat John had commanded in the wartime Pacific into an undeserved reputation for heroism. In 1946 his father intervened again, pushing John into his first race for public office. The father devised the strategy and paid the bills that secured victory for the novice and a place in the Massachusetts delegation to the U.S. House of Representatives.

That race marked the beginning of a fourteen-year campaign to win the presidency, inspired and guided by the father at every step along the way. In 1952 John Kennedy jumped to the greater visibility of the U.S. Senate after a sweet victory over a Boston Brahmin, Henry Cabot Lodge, Jr. With the White House the next goal, Kennedy hired a talented writer, Theodore Sorensen, who would ghost his speeches, articles, and prize-winning 1956 book, *Profiles in Courage*, and thereby cement his reputation for intellectual depth. He also took the wife, Jacqueline Bouvier, who would establish his image as a serious family man while adding to the aura of public charm and elegance already surrounding the Kennedy clan. After a warm-up shot at the vice presidency at the 1956 Democratic convention, Kennedy focused on the 1960 presidential campaign. He pushed past Hubert Humphrey and Lyndon Johnson to win his party's nomination, and then narrowly edged out Richard Nixon in the national election. Kennedy had become a knowledgeable and effective politician.

The man who entered the White House had serious personal problems. Still emotionally immature, he continued to pursue a playboy lifestyle that left him subject to blackmail from jilted lovers and dubious friends and that put his entire administration at risk of serious scandal. His incessant affairs, together with his frequent indifference to his wife, strained what the public took to be an ideal marriage. Kennedy was, moreover, hobbled by continuing ill health. Medication helped to keep him going—painkillers for his back, cortisone for malfunctioning adrenal glands, and a New York doctor's home brew (including amphetamines and steroids) that served as an all-purpose pick-me-up. But these drugs entered his bloodstream without being medically coordinated—producing effects on judgment and emotional stability that are difficult to measure.

Kennedy shared with his advisers a shallow understanding of foreign policy, never tested against practical, nuts-and-bolts experience with decision-making. The most pronounced feature of his foreign-policy outlook was a simple, reflexive anticommunism that was a core principle for Kennedy senior and a prerequisite for political success in Cold War America. In fact, in the late 1940s Congressman Kennedy had played on the dangers of domestic subversion, and that most infamous of Red hunters, Senator Joseph McCarthy, had become not just a political ally but also a family friend.

Through the 1950s and down to the eve of his presidency, Kennedy had defined the national mission in terms of a muscular defense of liberal institutions and values against the latest challenge, that of communism: "The American purpose remains what it has been since the nation's founding: to demonstrate that the organization of man and societies on the basis of human freedom is not an absurdity but an enriching, ennobling, practical achievement." As the 1960 election approached, he blamed the Republican Eisenhower for having lost Cuba to communism, and promised that he would do better, giving the world strong American leadership and America a strong military. He called for sacrifice—in the words of the well-received inaugural address (as usual, a Sorensen product), to "pay any price, bear any burden, meet any hardship, support any friend" to stop communism and defend freedom around the world.[6]

Vietnam had for a decade figured prominently in Kennedy's thinking. His tour of the region in 1951 revealed that "the fires of nationalism so long dormant have been kindled and are now ablaze." In Vietnam, as elsewhere, colonialism was doomed, and those committed to saving that country from communism, he warned the Senate in April 1954 (with the Dien Bien Phu battle in progress), would make no headway as long as their cause was tainted by colonial ambitions. With the French soon in retreat, he joined the circle of American Catholics promoting Ngo Dinh Diem to lead a free South Vietnam. In June 1956, before a meeting of Diem's U.S. supporters, Kennedy called for creating in Vietnam a revolution "far more peaceful, far more democratic, and far more locally controlled" than the communists could offer. By supplying capital, technicians, political guidance, and military assistance, Americans could "offer" the Vietnamese "a revolution of their own making." (The paternalism inherent in his idea of *offering* a revolution escaped Kennedy.)[7]

The eager Kennedy crew came into Washington in January 1961, already gripped by global Cold War imperatives. While standing up to Nikita Khrushchev, especially in a divided Berlin, took first priority, the newcomers did not neglect Southeast Asia. The new administration was soon humming with fresh activity and new ideas as task forces sprang into existence and inspection teams flew off for a firsthand look at that troubled region, above all, Diem's South Vietnam as well as neighboring Laos. But despite the hustle and bustle, the torrent of words and paper offering solutions, Kennedy did not in fact prove a pushover for a dramatic new commitment. Rather he moved at a surprisingly slow, at times even hesitant, pace.

Already waiting on the president's desk his first day in the Oval Office was the Vietnam problem that would recur throughout the Kennedy years—whether Diem would serve (or how he could be made to serve) as an effective or at least adequate instrument of U.S. policy. American officials in Saigon had already raised warning flags. Ambassador Elbridge Durbrow, a confirmed critic of Diem's autocratic style and his government's corruption and inefficiency, had won over the head of the American military mission, Lieutenant General Lionel C. McGarr. Together they were now proposing more assistance to keep Diem afloat, but only on the condition that he reform his regime in order to win popular support and make more effective use of U.S. aid.

Edward Lansdale, the well-known Vietnam expert, offered an alternative approach—treating Diem as a patient who would respond better to solicitude and good doctoring than to attempts at browbeating him into better health. A visit to Vietnam in early January 1961 had left Lansdale depressed. Diem seemed isolated and more dependent than ever on his brother and chief adviser, Ngo Dinh Nhu; the guerrillas were winning the countryside; and the U.S. military still acted as though it were facing a conventional war. In a report that made its way to Kennedy, Lansdale warned that Vietnam was "in a critical condition" and required "emergency treatment." The cure lay in a new team headed, Lansdale hinted none too subtly, by Lansdale himself. As he explained, what Vietnam required was "a hard core of experienced Americans who know and really like Asia and the Asians, dedicated people who are willing to risk their lives for the ideals of freedom, and who will try to influence and guide the Vietnamese towards U.S. policy objectives with the warm friendships and affection which our close alliance deserves."[8]

Kennedy responded hesitantly. How could he figure out what Diem and South Vietnam needed when Durbrow, McGarr, and Lansdale saw the same evidence and visited the same sites and yet came to markedly different conclusions? What was he to conclude when American representatives came away from meetings with Diem—clad in his usual baggy, double-breasted white suit and given to extended monologues—convinced the Vietnamese leader was inscrutable? The available information on the conflict in the countryside and especially on the nature of the enemy was variously thin, confused, and compromised and thus no more helpful. Kennedy was discovering that Vietnam was, for Americans at least, like a house of mirrors.

Compounding Kennedy's problem were the unpredictable, potentially unpalatable implications of the policy choices facing him. The United States could demand that Diem improve his government's performance as a condition for continued support. But what if he refused? Should the United States then withdraw and risk losing the region, or perhaps pursue an only slightly more attractive option—an international agreement to create a nonaligned government in the south? Such a government was not likely to last long, and thus the option only barely disguised defeat. Or what about a coup? Some senior officials were already advocating such a step to replace Diem with an able leader. But changing horses in midstream could be tricky and might even yield a successor regime no better, possibly even worse. The United States might then face a stark choice between outright defeat and an American takeover of the conflict. Or, finally, should the United States simply bite the bullet, as other officials were advocating, and move at once toward a greater American role in the planning and fighting? In that case, a coup would only make the task more difficult by adding to the turmoil. Better to work with the Diem regime, whatever its defects, and get on with applying American guidance and goods to the task of turning back the communist challenge.

A crisis in neighboring Laos complicated the picture and added to Kennedy's early hesitations. That crisis had developed suddenly, just as the new president took over the helm, but it had been brewing for nearly a decade. Anti-French Laotian nationalists, organized as the Pathet Lao, had cooperated with the Viet Minh in the defeat of the French, and after 1954 controlled several provinces in the mountainous eastern section of the country. From those bases, the Pathet Lao engaged in a three-way rivalry with neutralists and rightists for a dominant position in the country. In November 1960 the rightist forces seized power with the backing of the CIA. The Pathet Lao countered with its own military drive toward the capital, Vientiane. By mid-December the fighting was heavy, and by early the next year the Pathet Lao was making substantial headway against a disorganized central government backed by U.S. money and advisers (including some seven hundred military). The Pathet Lao for its part had the blessings and assistance of Hanoi and Moscow (including about five hundred Russian military advisers).

Meeting with President Eisenhower and his counselors on 19 January, just the day before the inauguration, the Kennedy foreign-policy team was informed that Laos was in peril and that the loss of Laos would doom the rest of Southeast Asia (consistent with the widely accepted domino theory). Eisenhower told Kennedy of his alarm over the situation. The outgoing president was, however, not clear what he thought Kennedy should do to avert disaster. The Eisenhower team probably relished handing the newcomers, so full of themselves and so critical of the Republican administration, a tough policy nut to crack.

Laos preoccupied the new administration for five months. At the peak of the crisis in March, Rostow argued forcefully for U.S. military intervention, and the Joint Chiefs of Staff reported that they could marshal at short notice an American force of about 60,000 equipped with nuclear weapons. The gamble that this force would stop the Pathet Lao and intimidate its outside patrons held little appeal to Kennedy, and so in April and May he moved toward his only other option, a negotiated solution to the conflict. Nikita Khrushchev and Ho indicated their willingness to cooperate in putting Laos on ice.

Despite the Laos distraction and the confusion over conditions in Vietnam, Kennedy had by then begun piecemeal to decide Diem's future. The need for a prompt, concerted, imaginative U.S. effort had been highlighted by a Khrushchev speech endorsing wars of national liberation, delivered in January just as Kennedy was taking office. Agitated by what seemed to be a fresh challenge issuing from the Kremlin, Kennedy had circulated the text of the speech to his aides to underline the test of wills in the making in Southeast Asia no less than in the Congo, Cuba, and Berlin. Kennedy had, moreover, responded favorably (along with Rostow and McNamara) to Lansdale's January report and had accordingly appointed a new ambassador, Frederick Nolting, with instructions to stop badgering Diem and to cultivate him instead. Also consistent with Lansdale's approach, Kennedy had called for more attention to counterinsurgency measures.

In late April and early May, with the Laos crisis settling down, Kennedy revisited Vietnam policy. The Bay of Pigs snafu, a badly botched invasion intended to topple Cuba's Fidel Castro, and the resort to a compromise settlement in Laos seemed now to dictate a strong stand in Vietnam if Kennedy was to repair his reputation for resolve. Within the White House, Rostow pressed for action, warning the president of the "extreme urgency of getting our Viet-Nam program moving with new faces, enlarged resources, and renewed conviction."[9]

In a burst of activity Kennedy and his advisers in effect confirmed the initial decision to stand firm in Vietnam and to work with Diem. Their main objective was now "to prevent Communist domination of South Viet-Nam." They would leave the issue of reform in abeyance (although Rostow reminded the president that the United States still needed to find a "technique" to get Diem and other clients "to do things they ought to do but don't want to do"). To dramatize his commitment to South Vietnam, Kennedy dispatched a high-profile mission to Southeast Asia led by Vice President Lyndon Johnson, one of the early flying-inspection tours that were becoming a hallmark of Washington decision-making.[10]

In private, Kennedy authorized more resources for both the U.S. team and Diem. He agreed to an additional one hundred military advisers (to reach five hundred by August) and the dispatch of four hundred army special forces ("Green Berets"), thus breaching the limits on foreign forces agreed upon at Geneva in 1954. He also agreed to help raise Diem's army to 200,000 in order to improve its chances against regular insurgent forces, estimated at about 7,000 at the beginning of the year. Kennedy even entertained talk of sending additional U.S. troops to bolster Saigon's position, but he would go no further than approving study of the issue by the Joint Chiefs of Staff. At the same time, he authorized CIA preparations for a secret effort in Laos to cut the main supply line running from the DRV to the south and for the dispatch of teams of South Vietnamese into the north on sabotage missions. With the administration having settled, temporarily at least, its commitment to Diem, Rostow publicly explained the administration's course in terms of the broad, abstract social-science concepts that had been his academic stock-in-trade. In a speech cleared with Kennedy before delivery at the U.S. Army's Special Warfare School in June 1961, Rostow contended that third-world countries such as Vietnam were moving through a "revolution of modernization." This inevitably unsettling process was marked by painful internal tensions and by a vulnerability to subversion, but it would prove ultimately beneficial as countries finally emerged "with increasing degrees of human freedom." To help new nations such as South Vietnam through their time of turmoil, the United States needed to promote social and political reforms, provide material assistance, and even send special forces and military advisers to block insurgencies led by communists, the "scavengers of the modernization process." The successes of counterinsurgent campaigns in Greece, the Philippines, and Malaya proved to Rostow's satisfaction that the communist "vandals," bearers of an "international disease," could be stopped.[11]

The issue of support for Diem subsided only to revive in the fall, as the Saigon regime's hold over the countryside eroded. Diem himself underlined the seriousness of the situation when in early October he suddenly requested U.S. troops or a defense treaty. To help determine his response, Kennedy sent an inspection mission to Saigon headed by General Maxwell D. Taylor and seconded by Rostow and Lansdale. Taylor was a self-possessed, articulate officer with a scholarly bent, who had crowned a distinguished career by serving as army chief of staff between 1955 and 1959. His criticism of Eisenhower's reliance on massive nuclear retaliation to the neglect of preparation for limited wars had won Kennedy's attention and an appointment in mid-1961, in the wake of the Bay of Pigs disaster, as his personal adviser on military issues. Taylor brought to his Vietnam assignment some Asian experience—service in Japan and China in the late 1930s and in

Korea during the last phase of the limited war there, as well as several visits to Saigon after the 1954 partition.

Taylor's survey led him to call for an ambitious program to save the situation. His most controversial recommendation was for the dispatch of 8,000 American troops to the embattled Mekong delta (to be justified, publicly at least, on the excuse of helping with flood relief). Taylor also proposed sharply increased levels of assistance and advice so that the U.S. Military Assistance Advisory Group (MAAG) could in effect function as "an operational headquarters in a theater of war." He wanted Americans to serve at all levels of the Saigon civil and military organization and assume the role of partner in running the country. Such a partnership would, he predicted, at once stiffen Saigon's backbone and gradually correct the serious flaws in its handling of military and administrative affairs. But, Taylor warned, redoubled U.S. support for Diem carried some risk of Soviet-bloc countermeasures, and Washington thus had to be ready to "cover action in Southeast Asia up to the nuclear threshold in that area."[12]

The irrepressible Rostow lobbied now, as he had since July, for vigorous action. He shared with Taylor the desire to get American forces on the ground. But he was ready to go a good deal further—to bomb Hanoi, perhaps seize Haiphong, and otherwise use U.S. military might to make clear to the North Vietnamese leaders and their Sino-Soviet patrons that the United States would not acquiesce in their ill-concealed effort to take the south. He urged the president to shed "the sickly pallor" of appeasement evident earlier in Cuba and Laos and to act with vigor and confidence against "a form of international banditry."[13]

Bundy lined up behind Rostow as Kennedy moved toward a final decision on the Taylor report. He was "troubled" that Kennedy seemed to be sidestepping the troop issue, which "has now become a sort of touchstone of our will."[14] The communists, he assured the president, did not want a military test and thus would not respond by escalating the conflict. Later on, if U.S. forces did not do the job of securing South Vietnam, then Kennedy could consider applying pressure directly on the DRV.

These strong recommendations put forward by Taylor and Rostow and endorsed by Bundy at last drew McNamara firmly and definitively from the margins into the center of Vietnam policy-making. When he had arrived in Washington, he had known nothing about the Vietnam problem. But its difficulty and its intricate mix of military and political issues were now to prove an irresistible challenge, one he would daily grapple with as long as he remained secretary of defense. As with his other Pentagon projects, McNamara approached Vietnam with the confidence that a hard-nosed, systematic examination of the issues and close administrative monitoring of the solutions would prove a winning formula.

McNamara at first reacted to the Taylor proposals with a perfunctory approval, but then—recalling what had happened when he had agreed to the Cuban invasion casually and with little knowledge—he decided to give Vietnam a closer look. Dean Rusk, who was reluctant to send U.S. troops to Vietnam before Diem had done more to help himself, joined McNamara in this reappraisal. On 11 November they submitted recommendations to President Kennedy that confirmed the earlier goal of saving South Vietnam from communism. To that end they called, first of all, for supporting Diem with higher levels of aid. The South Vietnamese government, the two policymakers argued, needed help even though it faced, by their estimate, at most only 20,000 "active" guerrillas. With the government in Saigon ineffective and the Vietnamese people seemingly passive in the face of communist terrorists, the United States had little choice but to do more.

McNamara and Rusk also called for an expanded U.S. combat presence, a recommendation that marked a significant advance over the policy of the previous May. In the short run they wanted to keep that presence small and unobtrusive and limited to units devoted to giving Saigon's military direct help with air transport, naval patrolling, reconnaissance, and intelligence gathering. These units would push the American military presence away from a purely aid and advisory role.

But looking further into the future, Rusk and McNamara saw the potential need for a more substantial U.S. combat capability and recommended planning for that eventuality. They were also ready to entertain the possibility of using "United States forces to strike at the source of the aggression in North Viet-Nam." At the same time they were clear to stress, as Taylor had, that large-scale U.S. involvement carried substantial risks. It might trigger a response from the communist bloc, thus forcing the United States into a prolonged war and into the dispatch of as many as 205,000 men. Or American troops might have to fight "in the midst of an apathetic or hostile population," and possibly without meaningful support from Vietnamese forces.[15]

Kennedy was unsettled by a war that offered no easy answers and seemed to require ever-higher levels of U.S. involvement. The prospects of making a dramatic troop commitment seemed particularly unattractive. When Taylor had delivered his recommendations on 3 November, the president indicated that he was "instinctively against the introduction of US forces." He declared to his advisers on 11 November, "Troops are a last resort." Attorney General Robert Kennedy, the president's brother and intimate adviser, chimed in even more categorically: "We are not sending combat troops. [We are] not committing ourselves to combat troops." To one of his White House aides the president explained, "The troops will march in; the bands will play; the crowds will cheer." But then, he added, "It's like taking a drink. The effect wears off, and you have to take another."[16]

On 22 November the president swallowed hard and accepted the McNamara-Rusk recommendations for at once stepping up the level of advisory and matériel support for the Diem government and for sending some operational units, such as helicopters and other aircraft to be flown by Americans under U.S. command. In exchange for this additional assistance, Kennedy wanted Diem to broaden his base of political support and improve the efficiency of his government. But pressed once more by the U.S. embassy on these points, Diem once more balked, grumbling over the prospect of becoming "a protectorate," while the government-controlled press unleashed a sharp attack on meddling Americans (described by one paper as "Capitalist-Imperialists"). Kennedy quickly backpedaled and settled instead for a face-saving formula that provided for "full and frank prior consultation" on all security operations. Kennedy's formal public pledge of support to Diem on 14 December was free of any injunctions to reform, while praising South Vietnamese courage in the face of a "campaign of force and terror" directed by Hanoi. Early the next year Kennedy observed, with a mixture of frustration and resignation, "Diem is Diem and the best we've got."[17]

President Kennedy was back where he had been on coming into office—tightly tied to the Diem regime. He had given no serious thought to a diplomatic settlement in south Vietnam, an approach he had used to extricate himself from Laos, and he had closed, if not locked, that exit by linking his name repeatedly in public statements and secret deliberations to the defense of that regime. He had set aside reform and instead decided to gamble that ample American aid and a robust American presence would carry Diem—whatever his defects—to victory. The establishment in February 1962 of a Military Assistance Command, Vietnam, under General Paul Harkins, a Taylor protégé, reflected the greater operational role Americans had begun to play and the need for in-country planning in case of a major U.S. combat commitment. Saigon got more sophisticated equipment, such as aircraft, armored troop carriers, napalm, and defoliants—all calculated to give an element of surprise and shock in battle. A genuine enthusiast for new counterinsurgency techniques and new equipment suited to tropical combat, the president assigned Robert Kennedy to join McNamara and Taylor in overcoming the resistance by the Joint Chiefs to this critical, if unconventional, style of warfare. As part of the counterinsurgency effort, Washington encouraged a campaign of rural pacification, the centerpiece of which—the strategic hamlets program launched in March 1962—was aimed at isolating the communists from rural support.

As Kennedy and his learned advisers devised a program in late 1961 and early 1962, the president formally gave its principal author the task of making it work. In December McNamara left for the first of a long string of high-level conferences held either in Honolulu or in Saigon to monitor the war's progress. He warned the attendees at this first conference that the war would have to be fought without clear political goals and with decided limits on military action. At the same time, the president moved Rostow —the enthusiastic advocate of escalation—a comfortable distance from the White House, to take charge of long-term planning in the State Department. Kennedy explained, "Walt is a fountain of ideas; perhaps one in ten of them is absolutely brilliant. Unfortunately, six or seven are not merely unsound, but dangerously so."[18]

Through 1962 and well into 1963 the new level of U.S. effort seemed to pay off. McNamara was getting from Harkins increasingly upbeat reports, confirmed by the statistics flowing from the field into Pentagon computers. Kennedy was happy to see Vietnam on the back burner, seemingly the scene of quiet progress, while he turned to fight communism on other fronts, most dramatically over Soviet missiles in Cuba in October 1962. However, the impression that this multiprong program was working and would eventually bring victory would be gradually undermined through the first half of 1963.

Ap Bac offered a signal that military training, new equipment, and a closer U.S. advisory role had not effected a significant transformation in the South Vietnamese army. As we have seen, the outcome of that battle in January 1963 suggested that National Liberation Front forces were learning to cope with the larger, better-armed, and ostensibly better-trained Saigon forces. But those at the top of the military chain of command running from Saigon back to Washington minimized the importance of the encounter. They argued that military advisers such as John Paul Vann were overreacting to the travails of the South Vietnamese army and thus were misleading eager young journalists such as the New York Times's David Halberstam, United Press International's Neil Sheehan, and Associated Press's Malcolm Browne. Critical press reports were simply missing the progress government forces were making. McNamara seconded this optimistic assessment after an April visit to Saigon: "Every quantitative measurement we have shows we are winning this war." (Rusk also professed optimism about political trends, announcing that same month that he saw a "steady movement toward a constitutional system resting upon popular consent.")[19]

But, in fact, the struggle in the countryside was not going well, for reasons difficult for McNamara and other high-level American officials to grasp. Hard numbers fixed in charts and lined up on graphs on the rural struggle were especially misleading. Much of the raw information on key indices of progress, such as enemy killed, villages secured, and supplies captured, came from Vietnamese commanders less concerned with accuracy than with making themselves look good and keeping the Americans happy. But even accurate statistics could not adequately measure the relative morale and motivation of the two contending Vietnamese sides or the peasant attitudes toward them and their respective programs; and thus two critical elements—political will and appeal —got lost in the analysis.

While American leaders could misconstrue the military and political struggle in the countryside, they could not blink away the collision between Diem and Buddhist protesters. That collision erupted right before their eyes in South Vietnam's major cities, ostensibly the regime's strongholds. Diem's last crisis began with a clash on 8 May 1963 in Hue between government troops and those celebrating Buddha's birthday. The encounter proved deadly, and it set off protests that spread in June to Saigon and other cities. Soon headlines in American dailies and pictures on the television registered sensational self-immolations by monks, dramatic government raids, and harsh language by Diem's sister-in-law about the barbecuing of religious opponents. At first, U.S. officials tried to put the blame for this public-relations embarrassment on irresponsible journalists, just as they had after Ap Bac. But longtime critics of Diem within the U.S. government felt vindicated, and even longtime supporters were deeply troubled by the way the crisis was further narrowing Diem's base of political support and distracting his government from the anti-communist struggle.

The most fervent of Diem's critics came together in a State Department cabal bent on stimulating a coup. At its heart was Roger Hilsman, Jr., an assertive Columbia University political scientist serving as assistant secretary for Far Eastern affairs. A champion of counterinsurgency, he strenuously argued that a government locked in conflict with its own people was already lost. Hilsman's determination to turn a new page in Vietnam enjoyed the backing of his immediate superior, W. Averell Harriman, as well as Under Secretary of State George Ball. They acquired in Henry Cabot Lodge, Jr., a critical recruit to their cause. Though humbled by Kennedy in the 1952 Senate contest and again in 1960 as Nixon's running mate, Lodge had nonetheless responded as a patriot to the president's request in June 1963 that he replace Nolting as ambassador to a troubled Saigon. The cautious, soft-spoken Nolting had failed to reform Diem; a firm, new hand was needed. Michael V. Forrestal—a young Wall Street lawyer taken under Harriman's wing after the suicide of his father (James Forrestal, the first secretary of defense)—served as the group's representative in the White House. Firmly convinced that Diem had to go, they moved with such unity and force that ultimately, if reluctantly, the entire administration was pulled along.

Diem gave them the ammunition they needed to act. Violating a pledge to Ambassador Nolting, Diem had had army units raid Buddhist pagodas in Saigon and Hue on 21 August 1963, arresting over fourteen hundred dissidents under cover of martial law. The U.S. reaction came swiftly. Within three days, on Saturday the twenty-fourth, Ball sent Lodge a cable responding to coup overtures made earlier by Diem's generals. Drafted by Hilsman and casually approved by Kennedy—then enjoying a weekend at the family retreat in Hyannis Port, Massachusetts—the cable indicated with marvelous bureaucratic indirection that if Diem did not replace his brother with better people, "then we must face the possibility that Diem himself cannot be preserved." Lodge, who had concluded after less than a week in Saigon that Diem could not win the war, responded on the twenty-ninth, "We are launched on a course from which there is no respectable turning back: The overthrow of the Diem government." The signals he had already sent through CIA contacts with restive South Vietnamese generals would in time produce the desired results.[20]

In Washington the anti-Diem cabal's bureaucratic coup at once set off recriminations and an extended and at times heated debate over whether Diem was salvageable and what alternatives existed for saving South Vietnam. The coup opponents, including notably McNamara, Taylor, Rusk, and John A. McCone (the head of the CIA), conceded Diem's flaws and the damage he was doing the war effort, but they saw no one better to take his place. Their suggestion was to confront Diem with a stiff ultimatum before following through with more drastic measures. Diem proved obdurate, flatly rejecting on 11 September Lodge's demand for Nhu's removal. Then frustration over the lagging war effort changed to alarm as Nhu talked of cutting a deal with Hanoi. Both Ngo brothers had grown resentful of American pressure for a shake-up of the government and the army, and, as patriots in their own way, feared American assistance was leading to American control.

Through the entire Buddhist crisis Kennedy showed himself perplexed about what to do with Diem. He veered first this way and then that, reflecting genuine indecision. In mid-June he had let the Vietnamese leader know through the embassy that a failure to conciliate the Buddhists and end the crisis would put U.S. support in question, and to drive the point home, the embassy received permission to build contacts with the opposition. While the CIA talked to the plotters in the military, the only group capable of overthrowing Diem and quickly putting a new government in place, Kennedy publicly called for patience as a country at war for twenty years tried to solve its problems, including now the religious dispute.

Kennedy's perfunctory approval in late August of a coup seemed only to deepen his uncertainty. At first he was angry that a policy shift of some magnitude had slipped by him, agitated that some of his most senior advisers were opposed to the shift, and disturbed that Lodge lacked General Harkins's support. But no heads rolled, and the president issued no clear, definitive reversal on the coup initiative. To the contrary, he seemed at first intent on increasing the pressure, stressing in a 2 September interview that Diem's government "has gotten out of touch with the people" and that "in the final analysis it is the people and government itself who have to win or lose this struggle."[21]

Kennedy attempted with Bundy's help to provide Lodge guidance on what to do with Diem, but in fact the secret cables he sent created a verbal fog. One, on 17 September, seemed to put Lodge on a leash. The time was not opportune for a coup; the ambassador should limit himself to a policy of pressure "to secure whatever modest improvements on the scene may be possible." Hoping for fresh insight, Kennedy sent new missions to Saigon. The first, led by junior representatives from the Joint Chiefs of

Staff and the State Department, produced two diametrically opposed reports, prompting Kennedy to wonder if its members had visited the same country. He sent another team, this time led by heavyweights, McNamara and Taylor. They returned from Saigon in early October to report that reform was indeed an illusion. Kennedy then authorized a dramatic aid cutoff, intended to make Diem reform but also serving as an unmistakable signal to Diem's generals of deep U.S. discontent. At the same time, he told Lodge that he was not to give "any active covert encouragement" to a coup, only monitor the coup plotters. Then a cable a few days later further muddied matters by telling Lodge not to discourage fresh leadership "capable of increasing effectiveness of military effort, ensuring popular support to win war and improving working relations with U.S."[22]

While his advisers debated and his options narrowed, Kennedy waited. Just as it took the State Department cabal to push him toward a coup, it now took South Vietnam's army to end the suspense. Conspirators led by General Duong Van Minh finally struck on 1 November. Diem's overthrow was followed at once by his and Nhu's cold-blooded murder in an armored vehicle after their being detained in a Catholic Church in the Chinese section of Saigon. The news left Kennedy pale, upset, depressed. He had toppled an ally. He had also lost control of events, with fatal consequences for a fellow Catholic whom Kennedy had once promoted as the best hope for South Vietnam. Three weeks later Kennedy himself lay dead in Dallas.

Diem's death merely served to accentuate rather than resolve the policy bind that Kennedy and his advisers had created for themselves by the fall of 1963. As deeply anticommunist as any of their predecessors, just as obtuse on conditions in Vietnam, and perhaps less prudent than the Eisenhower team, they had steadily deepened and expanded the American commitment. By 1963 some 25,000 Americans were in Vietnam. Some 16,732 of them were military "advisers," up from 685 in early 1961 when Kennedy took office. By the time of his assassination, 78 of those Americans had died in combat. Aid was now running at a $400-million annual clip. All this U.S. support had, however, not undercut the enemy, and Diem's collapse revealed that the policy of the best and the brightest had reached a dead end, forcing Kennedy to look for an alternative approach that would do no serious harm to his presidency.

The president had repeatedly heard from a variety of confidential sources of the increasingly grim prospects for the anticommunist cause. Those with some insight into Diem's sack of defects, if not Ho's bag of tricks, had warned that the formidable enemy would grind down the weak U.S. ally. Thus they had advised Kennedy to limit his commitment, even consider withdrawal. For example, in November 1961 in the immediate wake of the Taylor mission, Senator Mike Mansfield drew on his knowledge of Asia, where he had served as a marine in the 1920s, which he had studied as a history professor in the 1930s, and which he had thereafter followed as one of Congress's leading voices on foreign policy. He pointed out to Kennedy the multiple risks of putting American troops on the Asian mainland. Better not to militarize the struggle, he argued, but rather to insist that the leaders in Saigon embrace "the kind of political and economic[-]social changes that offer the best resistance to communism" and leave the main responsibility for preserving South Vietnam to the South Vietnamese.[23]

In April 1962 John Kenneth Galbraith, a Harvard economist serving as ambassador to India, delivered an even more emphatic warning. A quick tour of Vietnam revealed to him that the Diem government was "weak," "ineffectual," and perhaps "beyond the point of no return."[24] Pacification was doing more harm than good. Expanding the U.S. military presence would place Americans in a colonial role and lead to a drawn-out and indecisive military commitment. Galbraith's advice to Kennedy was to disengage by promoting a noncommunist, nonaligned government in Saigon acceptable to Washington as well as Hanoi and Moscow.

A skeptical intelligence community reenforced the position of dissidents such as Mansfield and Galbraith. From the fall of 1961 into early 1963, it handed down worrisomely negative appraisals at odds with the increasingly rosy picture drawn by the military. And while the government analysts turned positive in the spring of 1963, academic specialists and reporters were expressing an offsetting pessimism that intensified as Diem's political fortunes began their long, final slide. By the summer of 1963, once-apathetic members of Congress, newspaper editors, and other public voices were for the first time raising skeptical questions about the U.S. role in Vietnam.

Kennedy himself seems to have developed serious second thoughts about his Vietnam policy. In April 1962, with the war appearing to be developing favorably, he had casually expressed an interest in reducing the U.S. involvement, translated by McNamara in July into a clear order to plan for phasing out U.S. forces by 1965, though, to be sure, he made withdrawals contingent on continued progress in the war effort. Kennedy clung to the withdrawal option in 1963. On 6 May McNamara asked the military for plans for an accelerated U.S. phaseout, including preparations for removing the first thousand men. As late as October, with coup talk in the air, McNamara joined Taylor in affirming the thousand-man pullout, while professing hope that the war could be won by the end of 1965. On 2 October the White House made public the withdrawal (now scheduled for the end of the year) and indicated that most of the American military would be out by 1965. On 31 October Kennedy himself again referred to a limited, end-of-the-year reduction. Diem's death the next day seems to have intensified Kennedy's impulse to close out or at least downgrade the Vietnam commitment. On 12 November he conceded to Senator Wayne Morse, a critic of Vietnam policy, serious flaws in the U.S. approach, and followed two days later with a press-conference statement about wanting to bring Americans home. On 21 November, before leaving for Texas, a nervous Kennedy privately indicated a readiness to initiate in the new year a thorough, general review of the U.S. role in Southeast Asia.

There is, however, good reason for caution in interpreting this talk of troop reductions and a fundamental policy reappraisal. Kennedy's comments to this effect were intermittent, often couched in vague language, and frequently joined to calls to pursue, even intensify, the Vietnam struggle. For example, he vowed at a 17 July 1963 press conference, "We are not going to withdraw from that effort. In my opinion, for us to withdraw from that effort would mean a collapse not only of South Viet-Nam, but Southeast Asia."[25] Even later in the Diem crisis (on 2 and 9 September), he publicly and emphatically affirmed his belief in the domino theory, his preoccupation with winning the war, and his fear of South Vietnam's fall unleashing a Chinese assault across Southeast Asia. When he talked about getting Americans out of Vietnam on 14 November, he also called in the same breath for intensifying the American effort there. Even the Dallas trip, made with the 1964 election in mind, was to have been the occasion for a speech heavy in its emphasis on global anticommunism and military preparedness that was vintage Kennedy and that was distinctly at odds with any softening on Vietnam.

Moreover, we have to keep in mind that an order to plan was not the same as a decision to execute those plans. The U.S. military ordinarily planned for a great variety of contingencies, including major troop deployments as well as reductions. Even if carried out, a thousand-man withdrawal might have amounted to little more than a token of Kennedy's desire to bring the boys home at some undetermined time in the future, and could in practical terms have meant nothing if quiet increases in some units were to be offset by highly publicized reductions in others.

But it is possible that Kennedy was serious in the withdrawal plan and that he felt rising doubts about the Cold War approach to Vietnam. He did have a striking range of good reasons for rethinking basic policy. Not only had policy critics, both in and outside the government, repeatedly raised the warning flag. But political calculations also called for caution. Kennedy would not want to enter the 1964 election season as a president leading the country into a war on the Asian mainland. With unpleasant Korean War memories still fresh, the U.S. electorate, however anticommunist in principle, was not likely to welcome the prospect of American troops fighting in Vietnam. Kennedy may, moreover, have been personally anguished by the rising level of destruction within Vietnam and its toll on civilians. These concerns were evident in his qualms about the use of defoliants, napalm, and free-fire zones (although in each case he had finally given at least limited approval). Finally, the president may have remembered men who had died in battle by his side and under his command as a lengthening list of soldiers killed in Vietnam reached their commander in chief. Saving that country might mean the sacrifice of many fine men.

Despite all this, an exit from Vietnam would have proved for Kennedy an arduous and dangerous task. Part of the struggle would have played out within Kennedy. Quitting Vietnam would give the lie to the toughness and determination that among the Kennedy clan were highly prized traits. Perhaps more serious was his own resolutely anticommunist record. Was he ready to abandon a free people whom he had sworn to defend? Was he ready to face all the consequences that he had earlier predicted would flow from defeat—freeing the Chinese Communists to dominate the region, emboldening the Soviets to adventurism in Europe, and betraying the American national mission and people all around the world looking to American leadership? Was he ready to put in question his reputation as an effective cold warrior finally secured by his handling of the Cuban missile crisis?

Even if Kennedy had managed to transcend his cult of toughness and his anticommunist faith, he would still have had to face the prospects of a political firestorm set off by a retreat from Vietnam. Just as Truman struggled against charges of having "lost" China, Kennedy would have to face accusations of being the second Democratic president who had squandered an important piece of Asian real estate. He understood the special danger of being impeached by his own words. He had promised to do better than Eisenhower, who had let the northern half of Vietnam go. Kennedy had claimed he was ready "to pay any price, bear any burden." A retreat from Vietnam would allow partisan critics to picture him a weak-kneed appeaser who should not be trusted with the national security and the national honor. They would ask him to explain the terrible waste in lives and resources already spent for a cause he now wished to repudiate.

Anything short of victory could also lead to withering criticism from foreign-policy insiders. Kennedy could expect to hear from the two living ex-presidents, whose bipartisan Vietnam policy he had repeatedly, publicly, and formally affirmed but was now abandoning. Still others within his own party, the veteran cold warriors whose guidance he had respectfully sought at the outset of his presidency, were equally unlikely to suffer in silence while the communist bloc pierced the containment line and put all Southeast Asia and free lands beyond in danger. A reversal on Vietnam would also create dissension within his own already-divided administration, set off leaks of confidential information sure to embarrass the president, and lead to a possible loss of control over the national-security bureaucracy.

We will never know how Kennedy would have resolved an agonizing choice that carried costs and risks no matter which way he turned. The responsibility for choosing from an unpalatable set of options now fell to his successor, Lyndon Baines Johnson.

4

———

"THAT BITCH OF A WAR"

Lyndon Johnson loved folksy, vivid language. It came to him as readily in formal White House meetings as on the hustings in his native Texas. Not surprisingly, it repeatedly cropped up vis-à-vis Vietnam. In perhaps his most famous characterization, Johnson referred to Vietnam, from the perspective of retirement, as "that bitch of a war on the other side of the world." She had driven away "the woman I really loved—the Great Society" and with her "my hopes to feed the hungry and shelter the homeless" and "my dreams to provide education and medical care to the browns and the blacks and the lame and the poor."[1]

Johnson's remarks made Vietnam seem something that the Fates had visited on him. His words suggest that Johnson felt himself victimized—led astray by the allure of "the bitch." While this highly charged, gendered language tells us something important about LBJ's own style and outlook, it also obscures the critical decisions that Johnson himself made as he turned a war heavily backed by the United States into one actually fought by Americans.

The person who made those decisions was a Texas politician with deep agrarian roots, a strong faith in the capacity of the government to help people, a pronounced macho outlook, and, above all, an oversized, complicated personality. Any attempt to understand Johnson's role in Vietnam must go back well before 22 November 1963, the day of John Kennedy's assassination and Johnson's swearing in as president. The natural starting point is 27 August 1908, the day of his birth on a farm located alongside the Pedernales River deep in the Texas Hill Country, a distinct region extending just west of Austin of harsh, eroded limestone hills and narrow river valleys. A frontier backwater, still isolated from the rest of the state, the Hill Country could provide its inhabitants only limited education, medical care, and electrical power.

LBJ grew up on the family farm and in a neat wood-frame house in nearby Johnson City (the county seat named for a relative). Part of a large and extended clan, he was surrounded by grandparents, cousins, aunts, and uncles as well as four siblings. His was a comfortable and secure, though hardly affluent, childhood in which he was loved—and spoiled. LBJ's father, Samuel Ealy Johnson, Jr., was a sometime farmer whose love of politics secured him a place in the state legislature between 1917 and 1924. His mother, Rebekah Baines Johnson, was genteel, college-educated, and uncomfortable with the rustic Hill Country and the exuberant, gregarious, rough-hewn Johnsons.

From his father Lyndon acquired an expansive personality and the extrovert's love of the public stage, and from his mother the drive to succeed. No academic whiz kid who could match the best and the brightest, he was a mediocre student right down through high school. In 1927, after a period of wanderlust, he enrolled at Southwest Texas State Teachers College in San Marcos. It was inexpensive, accessible, and academically undemanding, and it kept LBJ in the protective, supportive embrace of his extended family. It was hard to imagine that this man with so unpromising a background would claim ever more powerful positions and prove a political genius with few peers in his generation.

Seedtime for Johnson began modestly enough—as an assistant to the college president and then as a schoolteacher in the small south Texas towns of Cotulla and Pearsall and then in Houston. In 1931 his emerging reputation for energy and political savvy got him a job as secretary to a newly elected Texas congressman. Johnson learned the Washington ropes, married Claudia Taylor (Lady Bird) after a whirlwind courtship, and then returned to Texas as the state director of the recently launched New Deal youth program. His record as an efficient, innovative, cost-conscious, and politically astute administrator laid the foundation for launching his own political career.

In 1937 LBJ made his bid for the House of Representatives by seeking an election in a district that included Austin and Johnson City. Although a long shot, the young, hardworking candidate won by associating himself with the New Deal programs helping the common people. In Congress he kept a low profile and steered away from controversy. He concentrated on serving his constituents, winning opportunities for his wealthy Texas friends, cultivating an ever-widening circle of contacts in Washington, supporting President Franklin Roosevelt's domestic initiatives, and in these ways preparing for the next step, a run for the Senate. He tried in a special election in 1941 but lost (his opponent stuffed the ballot box).

A world war diverted Johnson only briefly from his political climb. Following Japan's attack on Pearl Harbor in December 1941, he fulfilled a campaign pledge to serve in uniform. But by mid-1942 he was back in Washington, restored to his congressional duties. Johnson's almost demonic drive to master the political process and move up was leaving him increasingly impatient with the routine and the obscurity of his position in the House. Finally, in 1948, he got his second chance at a Senate seat, and this time he won, ensuring his victory by using the same ballot-stuffing technique used against him in his first run for the Senate. His financial fortunes were also looking up. Growing family wealth, based on an Austin radio station acquired with Lady Bird's money, allowed him to purchase a Hill Country ranch. It served as a refuge from the political pressures as Johnson began his rise to national prominence.

That rise was rapid. Between 1951 and 1956 Johnson became majority whip, then minority leader, and finally majority leader. By 1960 a fifty-two-year-old LBJ had reached a crossroads. He had suffered a serious heart attack in 1955, and knew from his family medical history that he might not live long. In any case, the Senate offered no new challenges. The choices seemed to boil down to leaving politics for business or taking the only political step-up left to him—into the White House.

The political course won out. But having vacillated over a bid for the presidency until July, he had to watch as John Kennedy quickly locked up the prize at the 1960 Democratic convention. Thus Johnson settled for the number-two slot, even though it put him in the disagreeable position of working for a younger man to whom he felt intellectually and socially inferior. (Johnson seemed painfully sensitive to Kennedy's good looks, Harvard education, aura of sophistication, and family wealth and influence.) Though the two men at least shared a passion for politics, they remained distant. As vice president Johnson served dutifully, with outlets for his formidable energies limited to promoting civil-rights legislation, overseeing the space program, and taking eleven goodwill trips abroad.

Unexpectedly thrust into the White House, Johnson took the presidency as a patriarchy—a style that he had learned in childhood and practiced in politics. He had paid his dues as a loyal political son—first to his own astute father, then to prominent figures in state politics, and later still to Sam Rayburn and Richard Russell, kingpins in Congress. Now he expected from aides and former colleagues the same deference and devotion that he had always shown his seniors and that was due a president. He was an often gruff, unappreciative, even harsh father, especially toward White House staffers, and he could burn with a smoldering anger toward anyone suspected of betrayal. He could on occasion be vulgar, manipulative, and a bully. But he had a warmer, paternal side revealed in token gifts, earnest solicitude for the welfare of the wives and children of his associates, and prized invitations to visit the ranch. Toward the public he brought a slightly softened patriarchal style. Like a kindly father certain in his sense of the larger good, he would patiently guide and cajole, always thinking of the best interest of those in his care.

The views on international affairs that LBJ carried into the White House were, like his thinking on domestic concerns, resolutely middle-of-the-road. Just as he liked to think of his domestic politics as guided by a centrist pragmatism, he associated himself in international affairs with the broad Cold War consensus on containing communism. For example, after Harry Truman took his historic stand against the Soviet threat to Greece and Turkey in 1947, Johnson lent his support. He explained in down-

home terms the dangers of appeasement learned by the democracies when they failed to stop Hitler and brought on World War
II. The United States had to stand firm because bullies, whether
communist or fascist, understood "force" and feared "courage."
"If I let a bully of my community make me travel back streets to
avoid a fight, I merely postpone the evil day. Soon he will try to
chase me out of my house."[2] In general, Johnson's foreign-policy
stance reflected the qualities he shared with his Hill Country constituents, neighbors, and relatives—national pride, a macho sense
of the importance of standing up to bad guys, a proclivity to talk
in terms of moral bromides, and a strong predisposition to support
the president and the principle of a bipartisan foreign policy.

Until his vice-presidential travels abroad, Johnson had had little
sustained exposure to world affairs, and those travels brought out
his strong populist faith in the capacity of the common man to
reach across national divides rather than a sense of the diversity
of the world. A spring 1961 trip to Asia convinced him that "these
Asians are just like you and I are, and that they share the same
hopes and dreams."[3] In his paternalism Johnson saw those hopes
and dreams cut from the American pattern.

Johnson's prepresidential exposure to the struggle in Vietnam
had been limited. Consulted in the spring of 1954 over the fate
of Dien Bien Phu, he had joined his mentor and fellow Senate
leader Richard Russell in insisting on "no more Koreas with the
United States bearing 90 percent of the manpower." Johnson had
not wanted to see Americans fighting on the Asian mainland,
especially to preserve colonial control. Later, in May 1961, he had
visited Saigon as part of Kennedy's early effort to beef up South
Vietnamese resistance. Johnson returned militant on the need to
stand firm in defense of the "young and unsophisticated nations"
of Southeast Asia, emphatic on the need to attack "hunger, ignorance, poverty and disease," and nearly apocalyptic on the dire
consequences of defeat.[4]

In a report to the president, Johnson praised Ngo Dinh Diem
for bringing progress and stability to his new nation and damned
the communists as "organized terrorists who roam the countryside." To win the struggle, Diem needed, in Johnson's opinion,
to develop the skills familiar to even a congressional neophyte,

above all, showing more concern with popular well-being and making his administration more efficient. Johnson was confident that by exercising "friendly personal political leadership," Diem could unleash the "enormous popular enthusiasm and great popular power" latent in South Vietnam. The Americans, Johnson thought, also needed to make more of an effort, getting into the countryside and promoting popular political, social, and economic welfare. At the same time, the United States could not let up in its military support, and LBJ could imagine even sending U.S. combat forces or providing air or naval support if Hanoi jumped directly into the fray in the south. South Vietnam was too important to lose, he concluded. A failure to act decisively could eventually compel the United States to pull back to San Francisco, adopt a "Fortress America" stance, and leave "the vast Pacific . . . a Red Sea."[5]

The moral landscape that Johnson had come to imagine in Vietnam seems derived from a Europe of the 1930s haunted by the specter of Hitler, while in the practical matter of devising a policy to create stability in Saigon and win rural support, he seemed to think in terms of his congressional experience and Hill Country folkways. How distant Johnson's Vietnam was from the real thing and how close to his own American experience is evident in his constant injunction to his Vietnamese allies to act like proper leaders—by which he meant helping constituents, showering benefits on them, and getting out for some serious handshaking.

Aside from his 1961 trip, Johnson was far from the center of Kennedy policymaking on Vietnam. His travels took him away from Washington during the critical November 1961 discussions, and no one thought to call him back in time to participate. Occasionally in 1962 he caught up on developments through reports from his military aide. In 1963 he played only a peripheral role in the decision to overthrow Diem. In late August 1963, immediately after Kennedy had authorized a coup, Johnson directly and forcefully questioned the wisdom of such a course without having first identified alternative leaders sure to prove better. He then advised, "Stop playing cops and robbers" and try to work with Diem. "It was difficult to live with Otto Passman," he explained, refer-

ring to the House of Representatives' troublesome, powerful opponent of foreign-aid spending, "but we couldn't pull a coup on
him."[6]

Precipitated into the presidency in November 1963, Lyndon Johnson inherited a Vietnam policy that had required an ever-greater
commitment of U.S. money and personnel. The upward pressure
for American support would continue, even intensify, as the political and military situation in Vietnam got no better following
Diem's fall; the United States would find itself still tied to a weak
ally in the face of an effective communist foe.

Johnson's response to the daily diet of grim news coming from
Vietnam was to persevere. His stance was in part shaped by Kennedy's advisers, men whom the new president quickly decided to
retain in his service and who had themselves begun the process
of Americanizing the conflict. Even more important, however,
were Johnson's own views and style. While Kennedy had shown
a marked reluctance to send significant numbers of American
troops to Vietnam, the new president was determined above all
else to win, even if that required a considerably greater U.S. combat role. This combination of old advisers and a new, strong-willed
president altered the policy equation. The momentous commitment that Kennedy had held at bay for nearly three years Johnson
would embrace in half that time. Johnson's choice for war—to
commit Americans formally and on a large scale to fight for South
Vietnam—would come not in one clear, dramatic, defining moment but rather in a series of four discrete decisions, each itself
reached incrementally.

The first of those key decisions came in Johnson's initial weeks
as president. During that time Johnson signaled a distinct change
in policy style, with critical implications for policy substance.
There would be no more of the Kennedy reserve in formal meetings, casual delegation of authority, and drift on reaching decisions. The new master of the Oval Office made clear he would
bring to Vietnam the same hands-on approach that he had always
brought to any important project. He would assign tasks, demand
a full team effort, and expect results.

Meeting with his advisers in his second full day in office, Johnson called for an end to "bickering" and "division" among Americans in Vietnam and made clear his disapproval of the coup against Diem. (Roger Hilsman, who had used the permissive Kennedy bureaucracy to promote the coup, was soon on his way out of the State Department.) After the meeting, the new president told an aide that he had to prevent the Chinese and "the fellas in the Kremlin" from thinking that "we're yellow and don't mean what we say." Vietnam was not going to wound him the way another communist triumph (the one in China) had hurt Truman. Johnson wanted his "fellas" in Vietnam to "get out in those jungles and whip hell out of some Communists" so that he could focus on his domestic program. He conceded that he felt like a catfish that had "just grabbed a big juicy worm with a right sharp hook in the middle of it."[7]

Part taskmaster, part cheerleader, Johnson left little room for ambiguity or hesitation on U.S. objectives in Vietnam. In that first meeting he stated his goal in terse, unambiguous terms—to "win the war." On 26 November Johnson made it official in well-worn Cold War terms: his policy was to help South Vietnam win its "contest against the externally directed and supported Communist conspiracy."[8] He would not waver on this key point through the difficult decisions to come in 1964 and 1965.

Within two weeks of his first critical decision—to stay the course in Vietnam—Johnson was already moving toward his second major decision: to launch a sustained bombing campaign against North Vietnam in order to save the South. First, he was hit by an avalanche of bad news indicating that the coup had not solved Saigon's political problems, and that in any case progress reported in the Diem years was illusory. Then McNamara drove the point home in a gloomy assessment offered on 21 December after a visit to Vietnam: "Current trends, unless reversed in the next 2–3 months, will lead to neutralization at best and more likely to a Communist-controlled state." McNamara warned of potentially difficult choices ahead. "We should watch the situation very carefully, running scared, hoping for the best, but preparing for more forceful moves if the situation does not show early signs of improvement."[9] John A. McCone, the director of the CIA, seconded McNamara's pessimistic appraisal.

Continuing political instability in Saigon did indeed keep U.S. policymakers "running scared." Despite high hopes among Americans for fresh energy and direction, the government established by the 1 November coup against Diem and led by General Duong Van Minh proved a dismal failure. The new regime was divided against itself, and Minh feared an intensified, more destructive war and resisted greater American control. At the end of January 1964 General Nguyen Khanh seized power in a shift sanctioned by U.S. officials on the scene looking for more amenable leadership. (For those who might have misread the Diem coup, this second overthrow made crystal-clear the consequences of defying the Americans.) Although Khanh would remain the dominant political figure for a little over a year, he sat atop a boiling political caldron. Intrigue more than ever distracted army commanders as they reached for political advancement and personal aggrandizement and in effect accepted their country's status as a protectorate wholly dependent on the United States for its survival. Increasingly, leaders in Saigon were less concerned with fighting communists (the Americans seemed determined to do that) than with controlling access to U.S. largesse flowing into the country. Repeated professions of cooperation in the common cause and constant lip service to reform would win Saigon not just survival but unimaginable bounty.

High-level meetings between Americans and South Vietnamese sounded more than ever like exchanges between impatient parents and irresponsible, unruly children. McNamara during his December 1963 visit had demanded that the new Minh government put its house in order, offered specific advice on command appointments and troop deployments, emphatically ruled out a neutralist course, and pressed Minh to speak to his people. Exactly a year later in an even more dramatic exchange, Maxwell Taylor, now the U.S. ambassador, bluntly berated Khanh for neglecting the war in favor of political intrigue and suggested a prolonged trip abroad. While Khanh protested that Vietnam was not a vassal and that Taylor was only an ambassador, Khanh would nonetheless set out on that trip two months later.

Johnson did not flinch in the face of the deeply troubling trends in South Vietnam. In a 1963 New Year's Eve message, he offered

General Minh an ominously personalized and public "pledge" that the United States "will continue to furnish you and your people with the fullest measure of support in this bitter fight." Lapsing into the kind of hyperbole that came naturally, Johnson described the efforts in Vietnam as a "war against the forces of enslavement, brutality, and material misery." At the same time, he denounced neutralization schemes floated in the United States and abroad as "another name for a Communist take-over." In an accompanying private message, Johnson characterized Saigon's deficiencies as at heart a matter of character and will. Minh had to realize that "he can magnetically rally the Vietnamese people if he will really try to do so."[10]

But Johnson did see in January, in only his second full month in office, that the short-term prospects for saving his client looked bleak unless he took some fresh initiative. Air power seemed the most formidable weapon in the American arsenal available to him. Its advocates reasoned that a rational Hanoi, threatened with heavy bombing, would stop its infiltration of men and matériel and shut down its southern operations. If the struggle could not be won on the ground in the South, then perhaps the United States would fare better applying direct pressure on the North. Walt Rostow, from his State Department exile, urged "a direct political-military showdown with Hanoi" rather than in effect conceding "Chinese Communist hegemony in Southeast Asia." The Joint Chiefs of Staff, also champing at the bit, recommended "increasingly bolder actions in Southeast Asia," including not just air, sea, and covert operations against the North but also South Vietnamese operations into Laos and "as necessary" even taking control of the fighting in the South and invading the North.[11]

As it became clear that more of the same would not bring victory, Johnson turned to Robert McNamara for counsel. The secretary of defense was the ideal Johnson subordinate—a hard-working, loyal, intelligent bureaucratic manager highly responsive to the president's wishes. After the very first Kennedy cabinet meeting, Johnson had observed, "That man with the Stacomb in his hair is the best of the lot."[12] Later, during Johnson's first weeks as president, the two had established a close working relationship. The president had then sent McNamara to inspect the war front, lecturing him, as he did others, on the need to press harder. Johnson had in turn been impressed by the gloomy report that McNamara had brought back. The new relationship—never a friendship—would last down through the critical decisions of 1964–1965 and beyond. Just as McNamara had sought to preserve the option of military disengagement for an uneasy Kennedy, he would throw all his energy into securing the victory demanded by a determined Johnson.

McNamara produced the critical consensus recommendation in March 1964 that squarely put the issue of air warfare on Johnson's table. He had set the stage by making yet another visit to Saigon, where the second of the postcoup regimes was still in the process of settling in. (While in Vietnam, he honored, however awkwardly, LBJ's instructions to get out and campaign with Khanh to make clear the U.S. commitment to "the people out there."[13]) On 16 March the secretary of defense reported to the president. He offered the usual reminders of how Cold War axioms applied to Vietnam. That country was the first domino whose fall would bring all Southeast Asia under communist sway and endanger Australia, New Zealand, Taiwan, Korea, and Japan. It was also a test of the American ability to defeat a war of national liberation, that specter raised by Nikita Khrushchev in 1961. It was, finally, a factor in domestic politics (a point McNamara delicately left vague). Moreover, he explained, conditions in South Vietnam were worsening as the communists extended their control over the countryside, as apathy and indifference gripped many Vietnamese, and as Americans serving there succumbed to frustration. However able, Khanh did not have wide appeal, did not control the army, and could fall victim to a coup or assassination at any time. But prospects for the future were not all bleak. Khanh and his associates were "highly responsive to U.S. advice," and the United States should sustain him with "all possible energy and resources." McNamara included in his long list of possible initiatives putting the direct squeeze on Hanoi by bombing.[14]

The day before McNamara's report, Johnson had used a television interview to signal his receptiveness to such a recommendation for stronger action. He made the obligatory reference to the domino theory, warning that "hundreds of millions of people" in Southeast Asia were in peril. "[W]e must do everything that we can, we must be responsible, we must stay there and help them, and that is what we are going to do."[15] The next day Johnson agreed to plan for air strikes. And two months later, once more following a whirlwind McNamara visit to Vietnam, he quietly issued instructions to lay the groundwork for bombing by beginning reconnaissance flights over the North and by drafting a broadly worded congressional authorization for the use of force in Southeast Asia. At the same time, the Johnson administration enlisted the assistance of a Canadian diplomat to send a warning to Hanoi: either cease support for the National Liberation Front (NLF) and, in return for ending the conflict and assuming a more nonaligned international position, receive U.S. economic aid and diplomatic backing—or face for the first time U.S. air and naval attacks.

But Johnson was in no hurry to bomb Hanoi. He had good reason. First of all, he hoped that Saigon might yet rally against the enemy. To that end Johnson continued to pump into the country money, equipment, and advisers (up to 23,300 by the end of 1964). Moreover, his caution was reenforced by the looming election. Johnson did not want to appear before the electorate as the candidate of war. He publicly spoke during the campaign in terms that positioned him squarely in the nebulous middle ground on Vietnam. While vowing to use American power "to whatever extent needed to help others repel aggression," he cautioned against the risks of escalation and promised (in language that would come back to haunt him) that "we are not about to send American boys 9 or 10,000 miles away from home to do what Asian boys ought to be doing for themselves."[16]

Finally, Johnson did not want a deepening conflict in Vietnam to imperil his Great Society program. He was pouring his incredible energy into some twenty major bills that defined that program and that would finally stand as his most significant domestic accomplishment. After reassuring a country traumatized by JFK's assassination, he had moved quickly to exploit the memory of the martyred president to push civil rights, a broad-gauge war on poverty, expanded educational opportunities, better health care for the elderly, aid to cities, protection for consumers, and new conservation and environmental-protection measures. Johnson wanted a mandate in the 1964 election to help him press forward on his still-uncompleted domestic agenda, and he did not want Vietnam to divide his supporters, derail his legislation, or give his opponents an excuse to call for budget cuts at home the better to struggle for freedom abroad.

In early August, three months before the election, caution suddenly gave way when Hanoi seemed to pose a dramatic test of Johnson's resolve. In separate incidents on the second and fourth of that month, two U.S. destroyers in the Tonkin Gulf reported attacks by North Vietnamese patrol boats. The first attack—directed against the *Mattox*, located thirty miles out—came hard on the heels of a South Vietnamese raid on the northern coast, itself part of a sustained U.S. covert-operations program aimed at adding pressure to Hanoi to change its policy. North Vietnam's military may have assumed that the U.S. navy was participating in the raid. Whether the second attack, reported by the *Mattox* as well as the *Turner Joy*, occurred at all is still a matter of dispute. Poor visibility and rough seas created uncertainties about an actual attack even at the time, and Hanoi has consistently denied launching that second attack.

Johnson took the first attack calmly, but he was galvanized by the second—by what appeared to be a direct, calculated challenge by the community outlaw. The attacks suggested contempt for U.S. power and resolve and struck at the most vulnerable point of LBJ's makeup, his sense of manliness. That outlaw needed a sharp and clear response. "Aggression unchallenged is aggression unleashed," he told the nation. Johnson moved quickly to prove that even "peace candidates" could defend the national honor, ordering his staff to pull from the file and rework the draft congressional authorization on the use of force. In short order (on 10 August), Congress gave the president a broad grant "to take all necessary measures" and "all necessary steps" to defend U.S. forces in Southeast Asia and stop aggression. (Only two in Congress, Senators Wayne Morse and Ernest Gruening, dissented.) But well before Congress had given the president a free hand to step up U.S. military action (indeed only six hours after the second reported Tonkin Gulf incident), Johnson had ordered American warplanes to strike against nearby North Vietnamese naval and petroleum facilities. Johnson exulted after the successful reprisals. "I didn't just screw Ho Chi Minh," he boasted. "I cut his pecker off." Johnson had proven his toughness.[17]

Or at least so he thought. But in fact Johnson's toughness—his warnings and show of force—had not moved Hanoi to settle on American terms, principally because North Vietnam was seeing things from a different perspective. Most important, Hanoi was, and had been for some time, encouraged by developments in the south. The tumult of Diem's last year—the collapse of the "strategic hamlets" program to make villages more secure and the Buddhist crisis in the major southern cities—had inspired visions of imminent liberation of the south. Spying an opportunity early in 1963, Hanoi had sent an increased number of cadres across the seventeenth parallel to reenforce southern forces. Hanoi discounted Johnson's attempt at projecting toughness; his bravado merely masked concern over an exposed and costly position that the United States had assumed in South Vietnam. In the autumn of that year Ho, as always with his eye on the least painful path to national unity, explained why he at least doubted U.S. determination. The Americans, he observed, "are more practical and clear-sighted than other capitalist nations. They will not pour their resources into Vietnam endlessly."[18]

In December 1963, just after Diem's fall, leaders of the ruling Workers' Party (the lineal descendant of the Indochinese Communist Party set up in 1930) had met for a major policy reassessment. Their conclusion was that the prospects in the south were distinctly favorable. The United States had on its side fielded a "henchmen's army." That force was not only demoralized and alienated from the Americans but also in irreversible decline. By contrast, the southern forces backed by Hanoi enjoyed improved "technical and tactical skills" and a heightened "fighting spirit" and thus could look forward to ever greater victories. Even if the United States chose to intervene more decisively, it could do no more than prolong the struggle. The Americans could not defeat the "14 million Vietnamese people in the South who have taken arms to fight the imperialists for almost 20 years, and who, with all the compatriots throughout the country, have defeated the hundreds of thousands of troops of the French expeditionary force."[19] Determined to press their advantage before Johnson could intervene decisively, the leaders in Hanoi agreed to widen the Ho Chi Minh trail to accommodate heavier weapons, to increase northern military forces, and to step up aid to the NLF. In April 1964 entire northern units began training for possible combat in the south.

In his first eight months in the White House, Johnson had done nothing to shake Hanoi's visions of an early victory. While things fell apart in Saigon and the South's prosecution of the war flagged, the NLF maintained its advantage in the countryside and made inroads in urban areas weary of war and resentful of heavy-handed U.S. intervention. Hanoi had been hopeful, at least down to the eve of the Tonkin Gulf clashes, that it might drive out the United States and reunify the country without a costly confrontation.

To be sure, Ho and his colleagues did recognize the possibility of a full-fledged American military intervention, which they assumed would take the form of an invasion of the Democratic Republic of Vietnam along with a buildup of American forces in South Vietnam. To avoid this worst-case scenario, however, they were not prepared to abandon the struggle for the south (as Washington demanded). Instead they focused on the neutralization option. The leaders in the DRV hoped that a negotiated settlement would in the short term remove the staunchly anti-communist government in Saigon and move the U.S. toward withdrawal. With South Vietnam effectively neutralized and with the NLF playing an important but not necessarily dominant political role in Saigon, Hanoi could wait patiently for a propitious time to reunite the country.

The DRV had promoted the neutralization option well before Diem's fall. It had praised the August 1962 international agreement neutralizing Laos as a model that might be extended to Vietnam, and an interest in this model may have prompted Ho Chi Minh to respond positively to Diem's overtures for talks in the latter part of 1963. Hanoi also responded positively when, between 1963 and early 1965, Cambodian leader Norodom Sihanouk, French president Charles de Gaulle, and UN secretary general U Thant each put forward proposals for talks intended to remove the states of Indochina from Cold War rivalry. When Premier Pham Van Dong received from a Canadian diplomat Johnson's ultimatum to capitulate or face bombing, the premier responded predictably by stressing neutralization. As late as April 1965 the premier would still be laying down peace terms that sought to breathe life into the 1954 Geneva accords and thereby eliminate the Americans as a force in a neutralized South Vietnam.

The U.S. bombing raids along the coast in early August 1964, coming on the heels of U.S.–backed covert operations against the North begun earlier in the year, convinced the leaders of the DRV that Washington had decided on raising its commitment. Meeting a week after the strikes, they concluded that the United States was shifting from "special war" (fighting through southern forces) to "limited war" (putting U.S. combat units directly into the fray in the south). But rather than give in to U.S. pressure, they decided instead to move the DRV toward a war footing and for the first time to place northern units in the south before U.S. combat forces began to arrive there. Early in the fall the first northern regiment left on the six-week march down the Ho Chi Minh trail, soon followed by two others.[20]

The Tonkin Gulf clash coincided with Hanoi's efforts to gain socialist-bloc support essential to sustain a battlefield test with Americans in South Vietnam and to deter an American invasion of the North. The USSR and China, although locked in their own increasingly acerbic dispute, responded by throwing their weight behind Hanoi. The DRV and China had earlier begun high-level talks on increasing the already substantial Chinese aid, which had taken the form of military supplies. Those talks had climaxed in June 1964 with Mao Zedong offering authoritative, sweeping assurances of support. The Tonkin Gulf bombing the following August confirmed his view of an imminent U.S. threat to the region. As a result, Beijing pledged to send ground forces to counter any U.S. invasion of the DRV; its troops and aircraft took up position just north of the border; and its military leaders began coordinating plans with their Vietnamese counterparts. By mid-1965 Chinese engineering and antiaircraft units (totaling some 250,000 men) would begin to arrive in the DRV to keep road and rail lines open, build airbases, and defend strategic targets against U.S. bombers. The troops, who would stay into 1969, freed DRV forces to go south to fight. At the same time, the flow of Chinese military supplies swelled dramatically and remained substantial down to 1975.[21]

Hanoi would be further reassured in early 1965, when the post-Khrushchev leadership stepped up the Soviet Union's contribution to the DRV's struggle. Moscow put together an economic- and military-aid program to counter escalating U.S. pressure and to prevent Beijing from becoming the DRV's dominant international partner. Notable items in that program were surface-to-air missiles (manned by Soviet personnel), advanced aircraft, and training for Vietnamese pilots.

In early July 1965, even while the Johnson administration entered its final deliberations on an all-out war effort, Le Duan (the head of the Workers' Party) would confidently argue that the DRV could prevail no matter how high the United States might escalate the struggle. While he estimated that the United States might commit close to half a million troops to the struggle in the south, they would be fighting far from home, on foreign ground where they were regarded as "an old style colonial invader," in a climate to which they were not accustomed, and against indigenous forces backed by both the North as well as China and the Soviet Union. If the United States sought to break the deadlock by intensifying its air war and even invading the DRV, then Americans would, Duan warned, not only face "17 million people in the North but will also have to battle with hundreds of millions of Chinese people." If, in desperation, Johnson and his advisers contemplated using nuclear weapons, they would have to face a collision with a nuclear-armed Soviet Union and an outcome that would amount to the Americans "committing suicide." The more risks Washington took, so the DRV leader reasoned, the greater the agitation among "other imperialist countries, factions in the U.S., and particularly the American people" and the greater the U.S. vulnerability to crises in other areas of the world. Duan's assessment of his foe was the mirror image of the Johnson administration's view of Hanoi: the enemy "is in a weak position and not in a position of strength."[22]

While Hanoi proved unbending, Saigon continued to stumble along. In August 1964, shortly after the American show of resolve in the Tonkin Gulf, renewed political unrest broke out when Khanh launched a drive to tighten his personal control. He encountered resistance from the predictable aspirants to power in the urban south—factions within the military, Buddhist activists, and Catholic politicians. Only in February 1965, when Khanh finally left the political stage, would Saigon begin to calm down. By June, his replacement would reemerge in the persons of Nguyen Cao Ky, a flamboyant air-force officer, and his army ally, General Nguyen Van Thieu. They would lead the regime in the south through its final decade.

This political turmoil steadily gave the lie to Johnson's remaining hope—that the South might save itself with no greater American involvement. American officials in Saigon were more somber than ever. For example, Maxwell Taylor, Lodge's replacement in the Saigon embassy, ticked off the doleful list of fundamental problems: counterinsurgency was "bogged down"; problems of personnel and factionalism increasingly plagued the South Vietnamese government at all levels; Hanoi remained determined in its support of the NLF, despite the high costs and limited resources; and the NLF remained strong despite serious losses. "Not only do the Viet-Cong units have the recuperative powers of the phoenix, but they have an amazing ability to maintain morale," a perplexed Taylor noted in regard to one of the enduring puzzles of the war for U.S. policymakers. He concluded, expressing a frustration widely felt among Americans both in Saigon and Washington: "[W]e are tired of standing by and seeing the unabashed efforts of the DRV to absorb South Viet-Nam into the Communist orbit against its will. We know that Hanoi is responsible and that we are going to punish it until it desists from this behavior."[23] In other words, it was up to the United States to alter the balance within Vietnam, now tipped decisively in favor of the North. What the leaders in Saigon would or could not do to defend themselves, the Americans would now have to attempt.

By late 1964 Johnson was in a position to make good on his threats to bomb the DRV and thus in effect to finalize his second major Vietnam decision. The successful air attacks in early August had set a precedent, preparing the U.S. public and calming doubters within the administration. In addition, Congress had not only gone along with the air strikes but also given the executive open-ended permission to do more; Hanoi had seemingly accepted its punishment and not struck back (as feared) at the vulnerable South Vietnamese regime; and Moscow and Beijing did not react rashly. Johnson's strong but measured response to the Tonkin Gulf attacks proved enormously popular and contributed to his landslide November victory over Barry Goldwater, a conservative Republican who had attacked popular government programs and taken a fervent anticommunist stand. Johnson could assume the powers of the presidency in his own right, with greater authority to push his domestic agenda but also to defend South Vietnam as he saw fit. In early December, having allowed a short interval after his election as the peace candidate, he moved to apply more pressure on Hanoi by bombing supply routes running through Laos. After a pause, he took advantage of a 6 February attack on the barracks of American advisers in Pleiku resulting in the death of eight men. The very day of the enemy attack, Johnson ordered 132 U.S. planes to strike three North Vietnamese barracks.

McGeorge Bundy played the starring role early in 1965 as Johnson moved toward a sustained bombing campaign. On 27 January he had joined McNamara in warning Johnson of a "disastrous defeat" if the United States did not use its power. Later on, the Pleiku attack had caught Bundy in the midst of his first visit to Vietnam. He reacted at once, calling for sustained reprisals aimed at undercutting the morale of both Hanoi and the NLF and correspondingly boosting that of Saigon. For Bundy, bombing thus figured not so much as a decisive step to quickly win the war but rather as a desperate measure to turn the tide of battle running so unfavorably against the Saigon government. He had found that government depressingly paralyzed by internal plotting, seemingly content to let the self-confident Americans handle the fighting, and operating under a cloud of "latent anti-American feeling." By contrast, the enemy showed an "energy and persistence" that puzzled and astonished him as it had Taylor: "They can appear anywhere—and at almost any time. They have accepted extraordinary losses and they come back for more. They show skill in the sneak attacks and ferocity when cornered." But rather than explore the implications of these insights, Bundy resorted to a non sequitur: "[T]he weary country does not want them to win."[24]

Bundy's bombing proposal found quick and general agreement among the president's leading advisers. Johnson now moved quickly to launch the long-contemplated campaign of sustained bombing against North Vietnam (known by its code name Rolling Thunder). By the gradual, controlled application of pressure, he intended to give Hanoi a chance to reflect and retreat before losing all its industrial assets, and at the same time he wanted to reassure the Soviets and Chinese of his restraint. Johnson would monitor the campaign every step of the way from a special White House war room. Each day he would himself carefully pick the next set of targets and then anxiously await the reports on "his boys'" safe return and on the precision and impact of their bombing.

Johnson thought of the escalating air offensive in predictable terms. It was not a brutal "rape" but rather a "seduction" of Hanoi into compliance with U.S. demands to end its "aggression." It was, alternatively, like a Senate filibuster that would encounter "enormous resistance at first, then a steady whittling away, then Ho hurrying to get it over with." What gender and politics didn't explain, frontier imagery might. "We have kept our gun over the mantel and our shells in the cupboard for a long time now," the president observed. "And what was the result? They are killing our men while they sleep in the night. I can't ask our American soldiers out there to continue to fight with one hand tied behind their backs."[25]

Even before beginning the sustained bombing campaign against the North, Johnson had already set the stage for yet deeper American involvement. The decisions to send U.S. ground forces to South Vietnam and to authorize them to play a combat role —the third of Johnson's major steps toward war—had begun to take clear form in late December 1964, when the president had virtually invited his team in Saigon to make the case for a significant U.S. combat presence. Doubtful that air power would prove decisive, he explained that he was prepared to make the difficult decision to have Americans fighting on the ground: "We have been building our strength to fight this kind of war ever since 1961, and I myself am ready to substantially increase the number of Americans in Vietnam if it is necessary to provide this kind of fighting force against the Viet Cong." Leaving no doubt about his position, Johnson cabled his Saigon representatives a month later: "I am determined to make it clear to all the world that the U.S. will spare no effort and no sacrifice in doing its full part to turn back the Communists in Vietnam."[26]

By the end of February 1965, with bombing of the North well under way, Johnson was ready to act. General William C. Westmoreland, since mid-1964 the commander of U.S. ground forces in Vietnam, was reporting a deteriorating military situation. The president responded by ordering 3,500 marines to protect the U.S. airbase at Da Nang. In early April Johnson sent more marines (this time to the area around Hue) and authorized offensive operations. The U.S. ground war had, at least on a small scale, begun.

Lyndon Johnson's speech at Johns Hopkins University the next day, 7 April, capped this pair of decisions on the use of air power and the deployment of ground forces. On the eve of the speech, the administration was already halfway committed to a full-fledged war, but not yet formally, publicly, definitively resolved. The speech made it clear that Johnson was moving rapidly in that latter direction. It came as close as he would get to the war message to Congress required by the Constitution. It warned of what was to come and why. Indeed, the White House staff put as much effort into the address as they would have for a formal request for a declaration of war. The product of a two-week effort, the speech had begun with drafts prepared by Bundy and two other White House staffers, Richard Goodwin and Jack Valenti. As the speech took form, Johnson himself got involved, rewriting the text, trying out portions of the draft on Walter Lippmann, congressional critics, and the press, and weighing the inclusion of a proposal for a billion-dollar development initiative that was to provide a TVA-like program for the Mekong delta as well as schools, health care, and food.

Johnson picked his time and place with a care that reflected his sense of the speech's importance. He had decided the Baltimore university was the right place, and so claimed as his own an invitation already issued to Bundy. But when the Canadian prime minister on a visit to the United States publicly offered advice on how to bring peace to Vietnam, an upstaged Johnson angrily delayed his appearance. After cooling off, he rescheduled the event for the seventh. Throughout that day Valenti continued to refine the prose and pare the length of the speech, while he and Bundy prepared the press. In the evening a serious, subdued Johnson entered the campus auditorium and spoke for thirty minutes into television cameras broadcasting nationwide and to an attentive audience, mostly students, every bit as solemn. He spoke with an intensity reserved for a major state address. There was no humor; only late in the speech did a hint of a smile break on Johnson's face, as he turned from the hard contest unfolding in Vietnam to his dream of peace and plenty.

The speech was vintage Johnson. It put the question clearly: "Why must this nation hazard its ease, its interest, and its power for the sake of a people so far away?" His answers amounted to Cold War clichés. The United States had to stop a brutal war of aggression stage-managed by Beijing against an independent country. Cold War commitments, the pledged word of American presidents, the fear of appeasement, and the hopes for a just world required action. He assured his audience that the use of American air power did not constitute "a change of purpose. It is a change in what we believe that purpose requires." But his disavowal of any "desire to see thousands die in battle—Asians or Americans"—could not obscure his determination to do whatever was necessary to save South Vietnam.

Mixed into the speech, as in Johnson's personality, was a progressive vision that made war a kind of madness, an affront to people around the globe who longed for peace and prosperity. If the speech has a claim to lasting importance, it is because of the way that it brought together and into the open the two irreconcilable impulses battling within Johnson himself—to serve and construct but also, if necessary, to fight and destroy in the name of what was right.

For centuries nations have struggled among each other. But we dream of a world where disputes are settled by law and reason. And we will try to make it so.

. . .

For all existence most men have lived in poverty, threatened by hunger. But we dream of a world where all are fed and charged with hope. And we will help to make it so.

. . .

This generation of the world must choose: destroy or build, kill or aid, hate or understand. We can do all these things on a scale that has never been dreamed of before.

Well, we will choose life. And in so doing, we will prevail over the enemies within man, and over the natural enemies of all mankind.[27]

Johnson's concluding remarks were both deeply moving and disturbingly naive. He would bring a better life to the people of Vietnam—on American terms. It would not be the first time blood would flow and bodies crumple in the name of high and humane ideals.

 The last of Johnson's critical decisions—the definitive, large-scale commitment of U.S. forces—came in a rush after the Johns Hopkins speech, unfolding with something like inevitability. Johnson remained determined in his defense of a Saigon government whose low morale was further shaken by the appearance of North Vietnamese units, while Ho would not abandon his lifelong commitment to national independence and unification. This profound difference now "put events in the saddle."[28] The phrase, one George Ball had used in October 1964 when seeking to hold the president back from military action, was tailor-made for the situation in which Johnson now found himself. The Texan was ready to mount up and ride off to rescue a Saigon on the brink of collapse.

The Johns Hopkins speech was followed by a flurry of White House initiatives. The day after, 8 April, a press release went out, revealing the earlier decision to place marine units in the Hue area. Over the next few weeks, the president began approving the dispatch of additional units. By mid-May the total number of American troops in Vietnam had climbed to 47,000 and were still rising toward the new ceiling of 82,000.

The tempo of the decision-making slowed briefly in May (in the aftermath of Johnson's decision to send troops into the Dominican Republic to stop a "communist" takeover there). He tried a secret one-week bombing halt to give Hanoi a chance to come to terms. The halt seemed to bring no response (even though Hanoi may have actually signaled a softening of its terms that CIA analysts overlooked). "Hanoi spit in our face," McNamara told LBJ on 16 May.[29] Two days later, bombing resumed, now more intensively than before.

The tempo picked up again in June. Encouraged by a new, permissive attitude in Washington and worried by enemy battlefield gains, Westmoreland asked on the seventh for still more troops. Johnson's response was to authorize both planning for the deployment of an air-mobile division and the beginning of B-52 bombing in NLF areas of South Vietnam (a decision made public on the seventeenth). Johnson explained to a visiting historian that he was not going to have U.S. forces "tucking tail and coming home." He would put pressure on Ho "till he sobers up and unloads his pistol."[30]

McNamara assumed his tried-and-true role of supplying the recommendation on which the president could act. The scenario was a familiar one: a hurried flight to Saigon (in mid-July) and upon McNamara's return a week later the appearance of a set of carefully framed proposals. In these proposals, dated 20 July, McNamara called formally for another, even larger round of troop increases—to raise the American presence from 75,000 as of that date to 175,000, with another 100,000 possibly to follow. While the president had already indicated his general sympathy for sending more troops, McNamara wanted him to go further—to intensify bombing, call up the reserves and national guard, raise conscription, and expand the defense budget. McNamara made plain that all these measures meant that LBJ would in turn have some explaining to do to the U.S. public.

Johnson was now ready to carry his string of Vietnam decisions to their logical conclusion. He immediately embarked on a round of discussions with his senior advisers, nominally to consider McNamara's proposals but in reality to give a last, extended examination to war aims and prospects for success. On 21 July Johnson met for three and a half hours with McNamara, Rusk, Bundy, Ball, William F. Raborn (the new CIA head), Earle G. Wheeler (chair of the Joint Chiefs of Staff), and Henry Cabot Lodge, Jr. (about to take up the post of ambassador to South Vietnam for the second time). The next day the president continued his formal canvassing of Vietnam policy, this time in a two-hour session with the Joint Chiefs, McNamara, and the other civilian leaders in the Pentagon. Finally, on the twenty-seventh, Johnson met with congressional leaders to bring to a close this extraconstitutional process of ratifying the decision for war.

As Johnson took his final steps toward war through the first half of 1965—from bombing to combat operations to a formal military commitment—the best and the brightest marched closely by his side. Walt Rostow, still on the sidelines in the State Department, continued to urge a strategy of victory over this communist insurgency directed against a free South Vietnam. He remained confident the United States could succeed in Vietnam as it had earlier succeeded in putting down insurgencies in Greece, Malaya, and the Philippines. The president, he advised, had only to bomb the North and stymie the insurgents in the South, and eventually Hanoi would have to realize that "its bargaining position is being reduced with the passage of time," and it would thus be compelled to accept defeat, an outcome the United States could encourage by offering "some minimum face-saving formula."[31]

Bundy, who had been shaken by Pleiku and sensed his boss had set a clear course, had become nearly as militant as Rostow. He praised the president for his willingness to escalate, urged him not to be deterred by the risk of a ground war with China, and pushed for intensifying discussions among his advisers on further steps. As Johnson approached his final decision on a major U.S. combat role, Bundy told him not to listen to the critics who saw the United States following French footsteps into a colonial war. U.S. policy was, in Bundy's view, far from colonial; it was, rather, supportive of noncommunist nationalists and intent on stimulating "a non-Communist social and political revolution." And while a tired and divided France had lost the will to fight on, Americans were, in his view, strong, united, and fresh. Finally, the United States fought not for self-interest but to save a country that would otherwise "quickly succumb to Communist domination."[32]

Dean Rusk, emotionally steady and uncompromisingly anti-communist, was serene in the justness of the U.S. cause. He had doubted the wisdom of bombing the North and continued to see the South as the critical battleground. But he finally embraced bombing and the dispatch of troops as desperation measures in late February, stressing to the president the importance of doing whatever was needed "to throw back Hanoi–Viet Cong aggression without a major war if possible." Faced with American bombers and troops, Hanoi and Beijing had sooner or later to recognize that the United States was resolute and hence to abandon an expansionist course doomed to failure. Publicly Rusk lashed out at "the gullibility" and "the stubborn disregard of plain facts" shown by professors critical of Vietnam policy. Could they not see that Hanoi was committing aggression plain and simple and that the failure now to meet the challenge of aggressors with their "appetite which grows upon feeding" would mean paying the same "terrible price" levied on those who failed to stand up to Hitler? To both Johnson and the American public Rusk insisted that appeasement now was sure to result in catastrophe later.[33]

McNamara, to whom fell the responsibility for overseeing this new American conflict, seemed oddly of two minds. He somewhat belatedly bemoaned the heavy military emphasis of operations in the countryside, and even expressed a casual interest in putting the Vietnam issue before some international forum for discussion. But he also showed an impatience for getting down to the details of winning. Hanoi had had its chance to respond, he told Johnson in late April. It was now time to act. The secretary of defense spoke privately with a resolution to match Rusk's. Abandoning Vietnam would produce "a complete shift in the world balance of power" and would have bad domestic repercussions, including "a disastrous political fight" and even erosion of "political free-dom." On the other hand, saving Vietnam would (he argued) have a range of benefits, including setting the stage for efforts at economic development and population control in a "gigantic arc from SVN [South Vietnam] to Iran and the Middle East, . . . proving [the] worth of [a] moderate, democratic way of growth for societies."[34]

Maxwell Taylor, the ambassador in Saigon and the only senior adviser with military-command experience, proved the most reluctant. A longtime opponent of Americans fighting conventional wars in Asia, he at first stood against the growing pressure to have American forces assume a combat role, even though he acknowledged that the contest in the South was going badly. The French had failed against guerrillas operating in difficult terrain, and he saw no reason to think Americans would fare better. But as LBJ went ahead with the deployment of U.S. troops—first to protect U.S. bases and then to operate offensively beyond those bases—Taylor, the team player, reluctantly went along. Better to fight than to admit defeat. He would not, however, have to stay in Saigon to help manage the Americanized war. He had agreed to serve in Saigon for only a year, and in early July Johnson announced Lodge's return as ambassador.

In late July Johnson had only to make a public announcement—a final ritual act—to bring the drama of going to war to a close. Johnson wanted to muffle the impact of what he had to say, so he decided to make the announcement not before Congress or in a dramatic special evening address to the nation but rather, without fanfare, at the start of a midday press conference on the twenty-seventh. The American commitment to Vietnam, he declared, had forced on him an "agonizing" and "painful" decision "to send the flower of our youth, our finest young men, into battle." He had resolved to dispatch 50,000 men immediately, raising the total U.S. force to 125,000, with more to go later (an oblique reference to the 175,000-man force he had secretly just authorized for the end of 1965). He was also increasing the draft quota from 17,000 a month to 35,000, while ruling out a call-up of the reserves.[35]

But otherwise a mournful and resigned president sidestepped the hard issues—even tried to obscure them with the simultaneous announcement of a Supreme Court nomination and the appointment of a new head of the Voice of America. Though pressed by reporters, he offered no prediction of how long the war would last and how many men it might take. Nor did he offer estimates of the cost—only a promise to consult with Congress as the bills came due. There would be no state of emergency, no economic controls, no new taxes to cover mounting costs, and certainly no stirring call to rally round the flag. What Johnson's formal announcement began, his responses to reporters completed—the clouding of the significance of the moment. U.S. forces would not seriously fall in harm's way, he promised. Their job would be to guard American facilities and provide emergency backup for Saigon's army, which would still handle offensive operations. He could see no reason why the continuing effort to protect South Vietnam should disrupt domestic prosperity. There was no hint of the long and costly struggle to come.

Johnson's decision for war remains today, more than thirty years after the event, the subject of considerable controversy. A brief, critical evaluation of four of the most searching and widely accepted indictments lodged against Johnson will help us better understand not just the man but the fateful process that set the U.S. course in Vietnam.

One frequently made charge—that Johnson was not candid with the public—is borne out by the evidence. During the 1964 election campaign, he downplayed Vietnam, pictured Goldwater as a man bent on leading the country into a dangerous conflict, and ruled out sending American troops. At no time between the election and July 1965 did Johnson offer a full and frank accounting. Indeed, as reporters began raising questions, first in Saigon and then in Washington, he did his best to cloak the meaning of his April decision to have U.S. troops play an active combat role.

Johnson's lack of candor is understandable. He did not want Vietnam to interfere with his domestic program. Nor did he want to create a war hysteria that might in turn give rise to a new Joe McCarthy or create pressure for a more confrontational Cold War policy. He feared an anti-Red frenzy that would create openings for crazies on the right and might lead the country into a wider, perhaps even nuclear, war. Moreover, Johnson felt as a Cold War president that he had considerable latitude in handling issues of "national security" such as Vietnam. During his long, formative congressional career, he had absorbed the prevailing notion that the president's job was to make difficult decisions and to educate the public and that partisan politics stopped at the water's edge. Once in the White House, he not surprisingly felt he had an obligation to lead and the right to expect national, bipartisan support.

Indeed, as Johnson inexorably advanced toward his July 1965 decision, the country seemed to be close behind him. His decision on bombing in February and on the major troop deployment in July enjoyed solid public backing. Congress also played by the familiar Cold War script, giving Johnson carte blanche to use force in Southeast Asia in August 1964 (the Tonkin Gulf resolution), and confirmed its intentions in early May 1965 by offering overwhelming support for additional appropriations to intensify the effort in Vietnam. Congressional leaders, regularly sought out by LBJ, just as regularly pledged their backing. Dwight Eisenhower as well as the "wise men," former foreign-policy notables first assembled by Johnson during the 1964 election campaign, also endorsed the war. Even the media played a consensus-building role by picturing Vietnam as the Johnson administration saw it—as part of the Cold War struggle.

But Johnson, an astute student of the public mood and political currents, had ample reason to worry that the deference usually shown the president in foreign policy was limited and that Americans might not sustain him over the long haul. Before the Tonkin Gulf clash in August 1964, almost two-thirds of the public knew little about Vietnam, and those who did were deeply divided over the best course for the United States to follow there. While the mass public had by spring 1965 become more attentive (with two-thirds backing LBJ's policy), politically engaged, outspoken, and influential Americans were already showing serious signs of disaffection. For example, the newspaper pundit Walter Lippmann began advocating a neutralized Vietnam in 1964. The editorial writers of the *New York Times*, including notably the respected James Reston, broke with the administration over the February 1965 bombing and recommended negotiations over escalation. At the same time, critics in the Senate began to speak out. By late March the campuses were also in ferment; faculty began to participate in teach-ins sharply critical of Johnson policy.

In case Johnson himself wasn't picking up the warnings, his advisers were telling him, as he moved toward a war decision in the first half of 1965, that public support was thin and brittle. For example, Bundy warned the president after the February 1965 bombing that "we have an education problem that bears close watching and more work." Over four months later, Bundy found the public "unenthusiastic" over the prospect of involvement in the Vietnam conflict. By late June, Johnson himself was worried that "it's going to be difficult for us to very long prosecute effectively a war that far away from home with the divisions that we have here and particularly the potential divisions."[36]

The evidence that the public was divided, disoriented, or lukewarm about Vietnam should have stirred LBJ's memory of the unsettling Korean War experience. Johnson had seen the country accept that war in 1950 and then quickly reverse itself. By the time of the November 1952 elections, the Korean stalemate had become an albatross around the neck of President Truman and the Democratic Party, and helped carry Eisenhower and the Republicans to victory. Johnson had in fact demonstrated that he had learned from Korea that the public had no taste for Asian land wars when he had counseled U.S. restraint during the Dien Bien Phu crisis in 1954.

As Johnson moved eleven years later toward a major commitment to his own Asian land war, neither the lukewarm public backing nor the political lessons of Korea were strong enough to check his forward movement or to get him to put the issue honestly before the public for an open debate. Prerogatives that he felt vested in his office and obligations carried by his country in world affairs drove him toward a definitive commitment without benefit of debate. The consequence was to create a credibility gap that helped destroy his presidency and fed a cynicism about politicians and the political process that is still with us.

A second common charge—that Johnson went to war blissfully unaware of the dangers ahead—is largely untrue. He listened to the doubts of a wide variety of critics (some more gladly than others), and then proceeded in full knowledge of the risks that he was running.

Johnson's politically savvy, longtime cronies were one source of warnings. Men with whom Johnson had worked in the Senate and in the national Democratic Party peppered him with cautionary advice from his first month in the White House, and their warnings increased in number and intensity as he approached his final decision for war. Some, such as Senator Wayne Morse (who cast one of the two votes against the Tonkin Gulf resolution) and Senator George McGovern, were annoyingly public with their criticism. (Johnson in fact seethed with resentment over open-press and congressional questioning of his policy.) Others, such as Senator J. William Fulbright (chair of the Foreign Relations Committee), Senate majority leader Mike Mansfield, Senator Richard Russell (Johnson's mentor and a Capitol Hill notable), Senator Frank Church, Vice President Hubert Humphrey, and Clark Clifford (a close adviser and influential Democrat), proceeded more discreetly in order to preserve their personal relationship with the president.

Mansfield struck notably early and often. In December 1963 and January 1964 he warned Johnson that the American people would not support "with blood and treasure" a wider war in defense of an unpopular regime. A year later Mansfield reiterated his call for negotiations because Johnson had to make "frugal use of American resources" and because a reunified Vietnam might actually serve U.S. interests as an obstacle to the overriding threat to the region, Chinese expansion. Otherwise, "we had better begin now to face up to the likelihood of years and years of involvement and a vast increase in the commitment, and this should be spelled out in no uncertain terms to the people of the nation."[37]

Between February and July 1965, as Johnson moved toward his final decision on a major troop deployment, the cassandras grew even more vocal. In February Mansfield argued against the retaliatory bombing, while Humphrey told the president privately that the public was "worried and confused" and unable to grasp how a "politically barren" appeal to "national interest" justified the risks and costs entailed in a direct U.S. involvement "in what looks largely like a Civil War in the South." In March, with U.S. troops on their way, Mansfield once more questioned the logic of a policy of escalation. In May Clifford contended that getting an imperfect Vietnam settlement would be better than getting into "a quagmire." The next month Morse, Russell, Fulbright,

Church, and Mansfield privately repeated Clifford's warning. Even at the very last moment, these insiders would not let up. On 25 July Clifford predicted to Johnson's face "catastrophe for my country." Two days later Mansfield spoke bluntly of a "vastly costly" war that would likely both escalate and lose public support.[38]

The most prominent in-house critic to whom Johnson listened was Under Secretary of State George Ball. In May 1964 Ball prepared the first of his major briefs in reaction against the administration's seemingly heedless, headlong advance into Vietnam. Once more, after the Tonkin Gulf reprisals and with what Ball recalled as "an unmistakable smell of escalation in the air," he attacked the notion that bombing was likely to resolve the conflict (drawing in part from a personal familiarity with the limits of bombing during World War II). Ball took the offensive a final time between April and July 1965, repeatedly putting before Johnson arguments against the dispatch of American troops. They would go into Vietnam as foreigners lacking local cooperation and good intelligence and fighting in unfavorable jungle terrain. Once casualties climbed, the prospect of national humiliation would close off easy retreat. Johnson thus faced a choice between paying "some short-term costs" associated with a compromise solution and "what may well be a long-term catastrophe."[39]

Ball rehearsed his arguments one last time in the lengthy meeting of the president with his team on 21 July. Virtually alone among the inner circle in voicing his apprehensions, he warned that, for the United States as with France earlier, "a long protracted war will disclose our weakness, not our strength." American troops would be fighting in a hostile environment on terms to be decided by the enemy for the survival of a weak and unstable government and would constantly run the risk of Chinese intervention. When Johnson worried about the loss of national credibility if he did not honor the repeated commitments made to South Vietnam, Ball at once responded, "The worse blow would be that the mightiest power in the world is unable to defeat guerrillas."[40]

Johnson listened to these critics, and in Ball's case he even encouraged in-house debate. He also knew backward and forward their concerns with the risks that would attend his deepening Vietnam commitment. Indeed, he fully accepted their call to avoid a provocation to China and the Soviet Union that might set off a wider war. He knew as well as they that the American cause was badly hobbled by an ineffectual ally, and he continued the search for ways to make Saigon both more popular and better able to defend itself.

Other points that the critics made he also acknowledged. He understood that the material damage inflicted by bombing, no matter how heavy, would not crush the North physically nor undermine its ability to support the insurgency in the south. He bombed to demonstrate American determination. He understood as well that if bombing did not intimidate Hanoi, the next step, sending American troops to fight, raised both the risk and the cost for his Vietnam policy. But Johnson could not end the bombing or withhold U.S. forces without in effect conceding defeat, and it was here that Johnson fundamentally departed from his critics. While some were prepared to countenance the loss of South Vietnam (usually in the guise of neutralization), such a loss was for the president simply unacceptable. He was not prepared as a person, as a politician, or as a policymaker to set aside the Cold War verities that had long given direction and shape to U.S. Vietnam policy. The conflict in South Vietnam, rooted in aggression by Hanoi, was a test of U.S. commitment and integrity, with far-reaching implications for the country's moral standing and world leadership. Thus some action, however imperfect, was absolutely necessary in Johnson's eyes. He made clear from his first weeks in office that he knew his mind on this fundamental point, and he gave no signs in the months ahead of second thoughts.

The third often-heard charge, closely related to the second, is that Cold War axioms obstructed Johnson's understanding of Vietnam. In at least two essential respects this charge is accurate. To begin with, neither Johnson nor his advisers could set the conflict in a Vietnamese historical context extending back at least a century. By seeing Hanoi's campaign in the south as part of a global pattern of communist expansion, the Johnson team almost automatically consigned its opposite numbers in Hanoi to a minor part in someone else's history, the Cold War drama dominated by the superpowers. Seen from this foreshortened, great-power perspective, the North was, in the president's view, just a "damn little pissant country" or, alternatively, "a raggedy-ass little fourth-rate country,"[41] and its leaders had to be made to understand that they could not win a test of power with the United States. A look at Vietnamese history might have suggested a people with a long, proud record of winning such seemingly one-sided tests. Cut off from the emotional, cultural, and ideological wellsprings of enemy action, American leaders suffered a failure of imagination and intelligence on the key issue of enemy outlook and resolve that was nearly absolute.

The dynamics of the rural struggle in South Vietnam proved only slightly less opaque. It need not have been so. American analysts did have immediate access to the rural scene, and they could supplement firsthand observation with captured documents and defector interviews to learn about NLF support, organization, and morale and hence about that organization's appeal and durability. However, general intelligence estimates made regularly available to policymakers at the top gave only limited and superficial treatment to the southern insurgency. More specialized reports did on occasion offer a strikingly perceptive analysis of the war for the hearts and minds in the countryside that challenged the simple, pervasive preoccupation with communist terror and peasant apathy. But such reports had limited impact, neutralized as they were by the volume of more conventional evaluations closer to the predilections of Johnson and his entourage and by the inability of those American policymakers to understand what was, for them, the totally foreign world of Vietnamese peasants.

A fourth and final, often-made charge against LBJ is that he was muddled in his basic policy—either that he went to war without clear objectives or that he erred in not making immediate, decisive use of the power available to him in order to realize those objectives. Here the record would seem to argue strongly in his favor.

Like his predecessors, Johnson had a clear goal: to contain communism in Southeast Asia. To be sure, Johnson as well as other, earlier cold warriors offered a wide variety of rationales for containment; they saw different enemies posing the main threat (Moscow, Beijing, and Hanoi); and they disagreed on the best means to hold back the red tide. But their ultimate objective remained the same. And though they had had to concede the loss of northern Vietnam in 1954 and the neutralization of Laos in 1961–1962, those two setbacks did not invalidate but rather re-enforced the case for Johnson to hold the line in South Vietnam.

While Johnson in his determination to stop communism did indeed draw selectively and incrementally from the formidable military arsenal at his disposal, he had good reasons for following this cautious course. He feared a conflict run out of control—justifiably so, to judge from what evidence we have on the thinking in Hanoi and Beijing.

More robust American military efforts, such as an invasion of the DRV, incursions into China, or unlimited bombing, might well have brought about precisely what Johnson feared and shaped his policy to avoid—a broader conflict and a higher price for Americans to pay. For example, any proposal to invade the North or to block supplies flowing south by placing U.S. troops on a line running from Vietnam's demilitarized zone across to the Thai border raised a long string of unsettling questions: Would Hanoi agree to fight the Americans on their terms or instead revert to unconventional warfare until the Americans grew frustrated and tired? To what level would Moscow and Beijing raise their assistance? At what point might Chinese forces intervene, or might Beijing try to spread U.S. forces thin by launching the long-deferred invasion of Taiwan or by prodding Pyongyang to raise the temperature on the Korean peninsula? How large a force would Johnson have had to field in order to meet these various responses? At what point might battlefield success by one side push the other side to the desperate, if localized, resort to nuclear weapons, and how far then might the combatants climb the escalatory ladder toward civilizational disaster? Johnson was neither a high-stakes gambler nor a fool.

Lyndon Johnson must bear primary responsibility for the Vietnam War. He advanced toward his July 1965 decision confident in his Cold War faith, his nationalist ideals, and his code of manliness. He proceeded deliberately, considering the risks that he ran in seeking to vindicate those ideals in Vietnam. He acted largely ignorant of Vietnam itself and with only lukewarm public approval. It is easy in retrospect to see the enormity of his mistakes and to point the finger of guilt.

But Lyndon Johnson's war was also America's war, a national crusade whose sources transcended one man. It reflected popular notions about national identity and purpose embodied in *The Ugly American* and a firm Cold War consensus amounting almost to a religion among the nation's best and brightest. It was the product of a string of formal presidential decisions, of which Johnson's happened to be the last. It developed under the aegis of an imperial presidency whose foreign policy activism had popular acquiescence and whose exercise of military power had slipped free of constitutional restraints. It had the blessings of seemingly knowledgeable senior advisers, notables of the foreign-policy establishment, and the vast majority of the people's elected representatives in Congress. Perhaps above all, it emerged out of an American culture which claimed to speak and act for other peoples without knowing their history, language, and aspirations. Coming to terms with Vietnam means a great deal more than coming to terms with Lyndon Johnson.

—∿∿—

HOW HEAVY THE
RECKONING?

In July 1965 Lyndon Johnson embarked on an undeclared war that would prove the longest in the nation's history and the most divisive of its twentieth-century conflicts. It would also prove a disaster to his presidency, to his country, and to the countries of Indochina. None of Johnson's predecessors in the White House—Harry Truman, Dwight Eisenhower, or John Kennedy—could have imagined how badly the Vietnam commitment to which they each had materially contributed would unfold. Any appraisal of Johnson's war has to take account, at least briefly, of the terrible train of consequences that his decisions unleashed and of the costs that they imposed on literally millions of people.

Even before his final decision for war in July 1965, Johnson had been getting indications that escalation might not settle the conflict but merely raise the violence to a new, inconclusive level. At the end of March the CIA reported that Hanoi had established a headquarters in the south as part of an intensified military effort. Here was the first hint, soon confirmed, that heightened U.S. pressure had not broken Hanoi's resolve. In the middle of July, on the eve of his definitive troop commitment, Johnson learned of a major Soviet military- and economic-aid agreement with the DRV. Hardly a month after his press-conference announcement of a sharp increase in U.S. forces, Johnson also learned from Robert McNamara that the war would require more troops than earlier projected. And the Americans would fight, Johnson could already see, with only token backing from some allies, such as Canada, Australia, and Japan, while Britain and France, both with hard-earned experience with the postcolonial world, openly opposed escalation and urged instead a negotiated settlement.

Before the year was out, Johnson and his chief advisers had no doubt that they were locked in an unpromising war. As usual, McNamara was the herald. He returned from another of his quick visits to Vietnam to report that the enemy was matching an increased U.S. effort with an increased effort of its own. He thus predicted that the Vietnam commitment would require still more American bombing and more American troops—a total of about 400,000 by the end of the coming year and perhaps in excess of 200,000 more in 1967. But even these forces, the secretary of defense warned, "will not guarantee success." He calculated that "the odds are even that we will be faced in early 1967 with a 'no-decision' at an even higher level."[1]

In mid-December Johnson shared his deep concerns with his stalwarts. He could see no sure sign that victory was nearer, despite the dramatic escalation, and his confidence in sustained public support in the face of a stalemated war was fast fading: "Our people won't stand firm—and will bring down the Government." McNamara agreed that the administration's calculations had been "too optimistic."[2] Though doggedly upbeat, Dean Rusk confessed that he could point to nothing concrete to support his more positive assessment. The best escape from this fix that the Johnson team could propose was a second try at a bombing halt. Perhaps grounding the bombers would draw Hanoi into talks. But the bombing halt, extending from December into January, proved fruitless; Hanoi was not interested in negotiating on U.S. terms, which still required in effect renouncing the goal of taking the south.

Johnson's fears were more than borne out in the months ahead. U.S. troop levels steadily rising toward a peak of half a million in 1968 did nothing to break the stalemate. Starting with the first combat unit to reach Vietnam early in 1965, U.S. ground forces had to face the grinding, demoralizing pattern of patrolling to clear the countryside. American soldiers sank into a disorienting and frustrating war without fronts, without a clear enemy, and without measurable progress. Patrols conducted by small units could bring some enemy contact (perhaps the crack of a sniper's rifle or thirty seconds of automatic weapons fire from ambush), a mine or booby-trap explosion, or an air or artillery strike by supporting U.S. forces on a suspicious target. The only certainty was the exhaustion of lugging a heavy load through enervating heat and moisture-soaked air across flooded rice paddies, marshes, rubber plantations, mountains, and jungles. The enemy returned to supposedly cleared areas, the patrols were repeated, and the casualty list steadily lengthened (to nearly 16,000 killed in action by the end of 1967).

What the survivors found on the other side of this initiation was (as one marine put it) "that cramped land of death, the front, that land of suffering peasants, worn soldiers, mud, rain, and fear."[3] Disillusion set in early, focusing first on the way the war was being waged. As the war dragged on from year to year and that disillusion deepened to challenge the very justification for fighting, soldiers turned their anger and frustration against political leaders, protesters at home, or the Vietnamese themselves. Those still compelled to regularly risk their lives (only a fraction of all who served in Vietnam) sought sanity and survival in tight unit solidarity.

While American troops usually experienced combat as relatively short, small-unit exchanges, encounters occasionally took on larger dimensions, as in the battles of the Ia Drang valley in November 1965 or of Khe Sanh in January–March 1968. General William Westmoreland followed the French in seeking set-piece battles in which he could bring superior firepower into play against NLF and DRV forces. Almost invariably, these conventional contests were American victories in the sense that U.S. forces held their ground and inflicted heavy casualties, but they proved in the final analysis as inconclusive as the small-unit patrols. The enemy faded away to recover its strength.

Johnson tried to extract some advantage from his arsenal of sophisticated weapons. He directed the aerial assault on DRV military bases, industry, oil supplies, transport systems, and infiltration routes. The air strikes steadily crept northward, flattening cities along the way and eventually hitting Hanoi and Haiphong. The tonnage of bombs dropped reflected the rising ferocity of the attack, increasing from 63,000 in 1965 to 226,000 in 1967.

Hanoi responded with countermeasures. It improved antiaircraft and civil-defense systems; dispersed industry, offices, and population; and created overlapping transport routes tended by large repair teams. As a result, the air war became extremely costly to the Americans, who had to spend something on the order of ten dollars for every dollar of damage inflicted and who eventually lost some six hundred aircraft in the effort. And while bombing disrupted life in the DRV and inflicted casualties, it neither broke Hanoi's will nor seriously impeded the flow of supplies. The most common popular reaction in the early years was patriotic anger, although the battering did eventually erode civilian morale. The bombing even gave Hanoi another argument to extract more aid from its allies.

Bombs fell even more heavily on South Vietnam, where they served to save the lives of American soldiers on the ground while harassing the enemy in contested areas. Already by 1967 the tonnage had surpassed one million. (Eventually, mounting totals for the South combined with those for the North—a total area less than half the size of Johnson's Texas—would push three times beyond the tonnage dropped by the Allies on all fronts during World War II.) B-52's were the most fearsome delivery system. Flying so high over suspected enemy positions that their approach went undetected, a formation of six such planes announced their presence only with the explosion of the first bomb in what rapidly became a carpet of destruction two to three miles long. Someone who had been caught on the receiving end recalled that "the terror was complete" as the explosions cut through the jungle like "an enormous scythe . . . felling the giant teak and go trees like grass in its way, shredding them into billions of scattered splinters."[4]

The costly, high-tech war took other forms in South Vietnam. Free-fire zones—areas declared occupied only by the enemy—were also carpeted by ground and naval artillery, while defoliants destroyed crops that might feed and tree cover that might hide the enemy. Great bulldozers completely flattened wide swaths of enemy-dominated areas. But the profligate expenditure of ordnance and effort proved as inconclusive in the South as it had in the North. It imposed impressive destruction but could not change the political equation, destroying neither the NLF's political organization nor its appeal.

The buildup of Saigon's army proved equally ineffectual. Though it had grown to a well-equipped force of 850,000 by 1968, it continued to suffer from low morale, corruption, and leadership rivalries. Even where Saigon managed with U.S. help to break the enemy's military hold, the government had difficulty winning rice-roots support. Close identification with a foreign power and the lack of a genuine, broad-gauge land-reform program undercut the government's political appeal, especially in contested regions.

Just as Johnson anticipated, this stalemated, Americanized war fed impatience within the United States and gave rise to the very political controversy and popular division that the president had sought from the start to avoid. Attacks came from both political flanks. "Hawks" such as Francis Cardinal Spellman, actor John Wayne, and labor leader George Meany wanted the president to make good on his professed determination to win. They demanded that he lift the restrictions on bombing or use American power in some other way to punish Hanoi and its Chinese supporters and thereby bring the war to a prompt, successful conclusion. "Doves," on the other hand, questioned the strategic wisdom and the morality of the war. They constituted a diverse coalition consisting of congressional critics such as William Fulbright (head of the Senate Foreign Relations Committee), celebrities such as Jane Fonda, Joan Baez, and Muhammad Ali, civil-rights leader Martin Luther King, Jr., the pediatrician Benjamin Spock, and cold warriors such as George F. Kennan who were disturbed by containment run amuck.

Dovish sentiment dominated the major public demonstrations from the start. A campus teach-in, held at the University of Michigan in late March 1965, inaugurated over eight years of national protest. The next month, Washington witnessed its first antiwar march. Protests followed in other cities in what had become by year's end a self-sustaining movement that would exploit a wide variety of techniques—from teach-ins and marches to letter-writing campaigns, civil disobedience, and draft-card burning. As the war dragged on, vocal antiwar activists dogged Johnson in his public appearances and picketed the White House. In October 1967, 100,000 protesters gathered in the capital and then marched on the Pentagon, where McNamara kept anxious vigil over the building's security as well as the crowd's safety.

Mounting opposition to this limited war began showing up in opinion polls probing a variety of key issues. For example, LBJ's approval rating had by June 1966 fallen for the first time below 50 percent, and by August 1967 it had fallen further (to 39 percent). Many Americans had come to fear that Vietnam as well as rising inflation and urban riots were pushing the nation into crisis. Polls dealing with Johnson's handling of the war also suggested trouble, with the disapproval rating creeping over the 50 percent mark in July 1967. In August the costs of the conflict (by then running at a $20-billion annual rate) became palpable to many Americans when Johnson levied a 10 percent tax surcharge on individuals and corporations. By the following October, 46 percent of the public—responding to another line of questioning—said that sending American troops had been a mistake, while only 44 percent approved. While fewer and fewer Americans supported Johnson and his strategy, increasing numbers responded in interviews with predominantly hawkish advice. Those favoring some kind of pullout were distinctly a minority (no more than 10 percent). The war was rending the nation, with young people, males, and whites most likely to be militant, while older Americans, women, and African-Americans and Jews expressed the strongest end-the-war sentiments.

In the face of adversity on the battlefield and at home, Johnson stuck to what he regarded as a moderate policy. He would not give in to the demands of the Joint Chiefs of Staff and other hawks to expand the ground war beyond the borders of South Vietnam or lift the restrictions on bombing. He would not play appeaser, a role sure to create havoc in Southeast Asia and perhaps beyond and set in question the American reputation as a determined, reliable superpower and global force for good. Nor would he allow Vietnam to destroy his legislative achievements, arguing that the country could have war and prosperity and Great Society programs all at the same time. Johnson later recalled his rationale: "After all, our country was built by pioneers who had a rifle in one hand to kill their enemies and an ax in the other to build their homes and provide for their families."[5]

This business-as-usual approach to the home front became less and less tenable. Resources were proving as limited as public patience. Soaring war costs were putting a budgetary crimp on Johnson's prized domestic programs, and the president's reluctance to raise enough taxes to fully cover the skyrocketing cost of the war after 1965 meant deficit spending that in turn ignited inflation. Johnson had gotten the alternatives right earlier in his Johns Hopkins speech—either destroy or build. Even a superpower conducting a limited war could not evade that basic choice.

Clinging to what he saw as the prudent middle way, Johnson railed at his critics. He blamed the press for alienating the people from their president. He struck out at liberals in his own party who seemed bent on discrediting Johnson in order to help Robert Kennedy reclaim the White House for his family. He attacked college professors for misleading youth with a naive view of the communists and with claims that "you can get peace by being soft and acting nice." He mocked Senator Fulbright, once a close colleague, as "Senator Halfbright" and "a frustrated old woman." Protesters were crazies and dupes. He tried to discredit them by getting the Federal Bureau of Investigation (FBI) and the CIA to probe for communist-bloc ties.[6]

As public support slipped dangerously, LBJ went on the offensive in late 1967. He sought to rally support by reminding Americans of the lessons of Munich and of the communists' global ambitions. He asked for signs of popular support that would hearten the men in the field and crush Hanoi's hopes for faltering U.S. resolve. He offered assurances of progress in the battlefield —what later became known derisively as the "light at the end of the tunnel."

The Tet offensive, an NLF surprise attack launched in late January 1968, forced on Johnson a painful reexamination of the war and a grudging policy adjustment. NLF forces with limited support from northern units took major cities, provincial centers, and district towns up and down South Vietnam, fought their way into Saigon and onto the grounds of the U.S. embassy, and held Hue for three weeks. The offensive dramatically gave the lie to assurances that nearly three years of direct action by the American military was bringing victory nearer. To the contrary, the NLF had challenged the Saigon government in its very strongholds.

Doubts became contagious, most critically within the administration and the foreign-policy establishment. The public, now more than ever discontent with the war, began to shift from predominantly hawkish to predominantly dovish.

For the media, too, Tet was a watershed. From the outset of the Americanized war, reporting had generally followed the U.S. government perspective. Like policymakers and most Americans, the media, including journalists in the field, had at first seen the Vietnam struggle through a Cold War lens—as a necessary response to communist expansion. Reporters' complaints were superficial, contesting not the ultimate goal of saving the South but the best way to do that. The first really profound doubts began to intrude in 1966–1967 as a result of contact with dissident policymakers, a foreign-policy establishment in ferment, and disgruntled soldiers in the midst of the fighting. Tet completed the process of disillusionment. While reporting in early 1968 largely conveyed the impression of a military defeat for the other side and continued to picture U.S. troops in a generally positive light and the enemy in negative terms, many in the media were now turning against the war.

While young Americans fought and died in Vietnam, the best and the brightest who had helped send them there began to decamp. By mid-1967 McNamara was deeply conflicted, distraught over the war and its effects at home but reluctant to abandon or betray the president. Johnson could see that his defense secretary lacked the stomach to go on, and in any case their diverging assessments of the war were straining their relationship. In November the president announced McNamara's transfer to the World Bank, a move handled so adroitly that McNamara did not know if he had resigned as secretary of defense or been fired. His successor, Clark Clifford, took over just as Tet was reverberating in Washington. Clifford quickly confirmed his earlier skepticism of the U.S. ground war, began pressing the president to shift course, and enlisted allies within the White House to sway Johnson.

McGeorge Bundy had formally bowed out even earlier—in February 1966—to take over at the Ford Foundation in New York. (To fill his place, Johnson arranged for Walt Rostow, that truest believer in taking a stand in Vietnam, to return to the White

House.) Bundy had, however, remained in touch as a consultant, and he was one of the "wise men" whom Johnson once again consulted after Tet. It was then that Bundy, along with a majority of his colleagues, precipitously withdrew their previously strong support of the Vietnam commitment. They told a stunned president that the war had become too costly to continue; it was time to find a way out.

Even Dean Rusk, the most durable of the Vietnam advisers, showed signs of faltering resolve after Tet. Never close to Kennedy, Rusk had established a good rapport with Johnson, founded on Rusk's absolute loyalty to the president and strengthened by their shared Southern roots and stubborn determination to prevail in Vietnam. Privately and no doubt reluctantly, Rusk now told Johnson that Americans, whose isolationist streak had long worried Rusk, had simply lost heart, and so he advised the president to seek peace.

With support crumbling even among his inner circle, Johnson decided in March 1968 to modify his policy. He began to limit the U.S. role in the fighting and to shift more of the burden back to South Vietnam's army (a strategy later dubbed "Vietnamization"). He thus refused to send General Westmoreland an additional 200,000 men. At the same time, he sharply restricted air and sea attacks against the DRV the better to draw Hanoi into talks that he hoped would bring peace and yet still preserve South Vietnam. At the conclusion of a nationally televised speech conveying these decisions, Johnson startled his audience by announcing his withdrawal from the upcoming presidential race. His public rationale was to remove his peace initiative as an issue in the coming campaign, but the withdrawal decision also spared a proud incumbent the possible humiliation of political defeat. Eugene McCarthy, one of the Senate doves, had mounted an unexpectedly strong primary challenge, which in turn had encouraged the more visible Robert Kennedy to launch his own bid for the Democratic presidential nomination.

Johnson's late-March peace initiative did not end the war. Indeed, 1968 marked one of the most intense periods of fighting, while the talks with Hanoi made scant progress. After opening in Paris in May, those talks first deadlocked over Hanoi's demands for an unconditional end to bombing of the North. Johnson's concession on that point in October still left the two sides at loggerheads over postwar political arrangements in the South and the presence of DRV troops there.

Nor did the presidential initiative calm the sense of crisis at home. First, Martin Luther King and then Robert Kennedy fell to assassins' bullets. The Democratic convention meeting in Chicago was plagued—and the nation shocked—by deep divisions among the delegates over the war and even more by violent clashes between antiwar protesters and the police in the streets outside. In the November elections, the Democratic nominee and Johnson's heir apparent, Vice President Hubert Humphrey, went down to defeat, narrowly losing to Richard Nixon because of the rift among the party faithful, Johnson's own lackluster support, and the stalled peace talks.

While LBJ ravaged Vietnam, it in return ravaged him, personally as well as politically. Worry registered on his cracked, sunbaked face. In January 1969 Johnson retired to his ranch, while the two remaining old Vietnam hands, Rusk and Rostow, repaired to university positions. In April 1972 LBJ suffered his second severe heart attack. He died the following January, and was buried in Hill Country soil, just as the direct American involvement in the war that bore his name was coming to an end.

In January 1969 Richard Nixon had assumed control of the deeply troubled crusade in Vietnam. He could see that three and a half years of direct American involvement had bloodied but not broken the enemy, divided the U.S. policy establishment, and then forfeited the support of the American people. But as a veteran cold warrior, Nixon could not simply walk away from Vietnam. Like Johnson and much of the electorate, Nixon wanted to avoid a humiliating defeat. During the election he defined his objective as "an honorable peace." In a speech given in May of his first year in office, he explained, "A great nation cannot renege on its pledges. A great nation must be worthy of trust." To abandon South Vietnam to its fate would be to impair U.S. credibility and prestige essential to its continuing to play a superpower role. As Nixon would later put it, "the world's most powerful nation" could not afford to act "like a pitiful, helpless giant" without encouraging global forces of totalitarianism and anarchy.[7]

During the presidential campaign, Nixon had boasted that he had a "secret plan" for somehow extricating American troops while also assuring the survival of a still-weak Saigon government against a still-determined foe. To judge from the course Nixon pursued in Vietnam during his presidency, his secret plan amounted from the start to little more than inspired improvisation, based on the familiar premise that Hanoi would give way to pressure. To keep the public and Congress in check and calm young radicals while he applied that pressure, Nixon announced what turned into a steady reduction in U.S. troops and substituted for the draft a lottery system to meet the falling needs for servicemen in Vietnam. While maintaining the Paris talks initiated by Johnson and supplementing them with secret contacts through his chief foreign-policy adviser, Henry Kissinger, Nixon searched for Hanoi's vulnerable point. He made diplomatic overtures to China and Russia, in part to temper Cold War tension but also to get the DRV's allies to promote a compromise settlement (much as they had done in 1954 at Geneva). In case Hanoi doubted his resolve (hardly conveyed by the daily spectacle of departing troops), he threatened new, powerful blows if a satisfactory agreement was not forthcoming.

By mid-1969 Nixon's strategy was already in trouble. The peace talks were getting nowhere. DRV leaders, whom Nixon as well as Kissinger were coming to regard impatiently as "fanatics," were not giving ground. At home Nixon's approval ratings were falling; critics were once more speaking out; and large demonstrations were resuming, with a nationwide protest in October followed the next month by half a million people mobilized in a "march against death" in Washington.

Nixon's immediate response was to emphasize Vietnamization, strengthening Saigon's armed forces so that they could take up the slack left by departing U.S. combat troops. Those forces increased to a million men (including an air force on its way to becoming the fourth largest in the world). Nixon also publicly attacked the peace movement, appealed to the "silent majority" for support against radical agitators, and quietly intensified the effort begun by Johnson to get FBI and CIA help in discrediting protesters and even moderate critics.

Looking for a new pressure point, the president turned to Cambodia. Under the cover of that country's neutrality, the DRV had safely marched men and supplies to the south, and its forces had repaired there for rest and resupply without worry about attack. Soon after coming into office, Nixon had launched a secret B-52 bombing campaign, beginning along the border and then extending deeper into the interior. In March 1970 the overthrow of Norodom Sihanouk, Cambodia's leader since independence in 1954, created a fresh opportunity for action. The coup not only destroyed the last vestiges of the neutrality that Sihanouk had tried to maintain but provided a pro–U.S. ally in the person of General Lon Nol, the former Sihanouk aide who led the coup. In late April Nixon approved the invasion long favored by the U.S. military. A U.S.–South Vietnamese force of 80,000 struck into Cambodia, with the ostensible target the DRV's mobile military headquarters there.

Nixon had taken a costly gamble. No headquarters was found. Cambodia was plunged into a double maelstrom, as the new U.S.–backed government in Phnom Penh threw itself into the destructive American-Vietnamese contest while its Khmer Rouge opposition, led by Pol Pot, gained momentum in the countryside and built toward a deadly social revolution. More worrisome to Nixon was the maelstrom of protest at home set off by the invasion. Campuses erupted from coast to coast, many for the first time, and at Kent State, in an act that produced reactions of horror around the country, the National Guard fired on student demonstrators, killing four. While protesters headed for the capital, Congress voted to revoke the Tonkin Gulf resolution's grant of authority to the president, and some members were calling for stronger measures to force an end to the war.

Nixon was drifting into a siege mentality. He felt beset by enemies in Congress, a "liberal" press, and the antiwar movement. He demanded a more active effort to keep track of this dangerous coalition of forces arrayed against him and, where possible, to discredit them. (The Watergate break-in committed by White House "plumbers"—so called because their job was to stop leaks

of inside information—was but one part of this broader effort.)
Even the public was slipping away. An all-time high of 71 percent
in the summer of 1971 called the war a mistake, and 58 percent
condemned it as "immoral." Meanwhile, disaffection was spreading to U.S. forces, who much preferred survival to becoming
among the last casualties in a lost war. Tensions within units ate
at the fabric of cohesion and effectiveness. Insubordination, killing of overenthusiastic leaders (a practice known as fragging), ra-
cial conflict, and drug use reached alarming proportions.

Nixon returned to his carrot-and-stick strategy in 1971, now
worried over his reelection chances. In February he sent an invasion force into Laos, hoping to cut off the supplies moving
down the Ho Chi Minh trail. But this stick, consisting of South
Vietnamese troops backed by U.S. advisers and air support, proved
brittle. DRV units quickly broke the invaders and sent them
fleeing home in confusion. The carrot, a comprehensive peace
agreement offered by Henry Kissinger to his North Vietnamese
negotiating partner, Le Duc Tho, in May 1971, did not prove
appetizing. Nixon dropped insistence on the withdrawal of northern troops from South Vietnam, but Hanoi would still not budge
from its insistence on Nguyen Van Thieu's removal from power.

It was now the DRV's turn to try to break the deadlock. In
March 1972 northern units launched an offensive in the Central
Highlands. Only 6,000 U.S. combat troops remained in Vietnam,
and public opposition and the approaching election prevented
Nixon from committing additional U.S. forces. But he retaliated
in other ways—mining Haiphong harbor, setting up a naval block-
ade of the DRV's coast, intensifying bombing of the North, and
hitting the advancing enemy in South Vietnam with American air
power.

Once the DRV's offensive stalled, attention returned to the
peace table. Hanoi now conceded that Thieu could remain in
power, while the United States bowed to the NLF's playing a
postwar role and to northern troops remaining in the South. The
resulting deal, formalized in October 1972, encountered stiff resistance from Saigon, and rather than force his ally to accept,
Nixon instead asked Hanoi for fresh concessions. (The nomination of George McGovern, a weak Democratic candidate, may
have eased Nixon's fears that getting a peace agreement con-

cluded was critical to his reelection.) Hanoi refused further substantive changes. Nixon retaliated with an intense twelve days of "Christmas bombing," including strikes on Hanoi and Haiphong at the cost of twenty-six U.S. aircraft, including fifteen B-52's. Nixon's decision provoked outrage in the United States and abroad. Hanoi held firm. On 23 January Nixon concluded a peace accord that differed hardly a whit from the October agreement. This time he imposed the accord on Thieu, sweetened with the promise of U.S. rescue if DRV forces remaining in South Vietnam went on the offensive. As an inducement to Hanoi to pursue a peaceful, political path toward reunification, Nixon promised $4.75 billion in reconstruction aid, contingent on the North's good behavior.

The contradictions within South Vietnam, sustained if not created by two decades of ever-deepening American involvement, at last moved toward resolution. No more than Eisenhower, Kennedy, or Johnson, Nixon was not an alchemist who could turn base metal into gold—or instill in the Saigon regime either the determination to fight toe-to-toe with DRV units or the capacity to win widespread support, especially in the countryside. Hanoi was, on the other hand, resolute despite the physical and psychological battering inflicted by a conflict running intermittently for over three decades. NLF units and activists had been badly hurt by the pounding they had taken during the 1968 Tet gamble, forcing regular DRV units to carry the military burden thereafter, while in the North heavy loss of life, especially among those sent south to save their brethren, was giving rise to draft evasion and disaffection. But Hanoi could still tap a determination to avenge family losses and a patriotic spirit of sacrifice. A southerner who served as an officer in the northern army and who later fled Vietnam observed that "you can't really fight without hatred." He explained what American policymakers had learned the hard way: "We had such hatred for the enemy and such devotion to the noble cause of liberating our suppressed people that we felt we could overcome any difficulty and make any sacrifice."[8]

The end came within less than three years of the Paris agreement. After waiting for the Americans to disengage and taking time to regroup and resupply, Hanoi launched an offensive in March 1975. What began as an effort to secure final victory within two years turned into a rout, with Saigon falling late the next month. As panic gripped its forces in the Central Highlands and rapidly spread south, the pseudo-nation of South Vietnam, abandoned by its American patrons, simply evaporated (or, more accurately, collapsed, like the dominoes once so much on the minds of American policymakers). General Duong Van Minh, the leader of the anti-Diem coup now returned briefly to power, surrendered to a victorious peasant army marching virtually unopposed into a city littered with hastily discarded U.S.–supplied equipment. Many senior government officials and officers had by then fled, scrambling out with the Americans into an exile they had prepared against by socking money away in foreign banks and by sending family members abroad to live and study. Those who had fought on the other side felt a joy and sense of fulfillment expressed in a poem cabled by Le Duc Tho to Hanoi from the fallen city:

> *Ah, these tears shed for happiness,*
> *This joy savored*
> *Only once in one's life.*[9]

Washington watched this last act of the war impotently. Discredited by Watergate scandals, Nixon had resigned in August 1974. His successor, Gerald Ford, had had his hands tied by a pervasive desire among Americans to banish Vietnam from memory. (Even admitting to the United States Vietnamese refugees who had served as allies encountered opposition.) Moreover, Congress was in no mood to rush to Saigon's rescue. It had already revealed its preferences by cutting off funding for the Cambodian bombing in mid-1973, reducing aid to South Vietnam from $1.4 billion to half that figure in 1974, and in general by whittling away at presidential powers in foreign affairs. Americans had had enough of Vietnam and perhaps even of the Cold War attitudes that had taken them there.

William Shakespeare's *Henry V* has an English soldier about to face a superior French force remark grimly on the mayhem to come and the responsibility borne by leaders whose embrace of war produces that mayhem:

[I]f the cause be not good, the King himself hath a heavy reckoning to make, when all those legs and arms and heads, chopped off in a battle, shall join together at the latter day and cry all, "We died at such a place"; some swearing, some crying for a surgeon, some upon their wives left poor behind them, some upon the debts they owe, some upon their children rawly left. I am afeard there are few die well that die in a battle.

This eloquent call from the ranks directs our attention to the "heavy reckoning" to which leaders, foremost Lyndon Johnson in this case, must submit.

In Vietnam an estimated 1.4 million—civilians as well as combatants on one side or the other—died during the U.S. combat phase of the war (1965 through 1972), and another 300,000 fell in the subsequent period down to April 1975. (Of these deaths perhaps only about 50,000 were the result of the controversial bombing of the North.) Saigon's forces alone suffered a total of 220,000 killed. By 1972 South Vietnam, with a population short of eighteen million, may have had a total of over ten million refugees. By the war's end a united Vietnam had 300,000 combatants lost without trace, some 1.4 million disabled and half a million orphans to care for, and schools, hospitals, and other public facilities to rebuild. The environment, especially in the South, had suffered long-term damage from the concentrated, even stupefying, application of U.S. ordnance (some fifteen million tons down to 1972) and from extensive spraying of herbicides (nineteen million gallons, well over half deadly dioxins). Unexploded bombs and shells seeded the soil both north and south.

While postwar Vietnam escaped the bloodbath that some had predicted, unification still proved a rocky road for a leadership good at struggle but less skillful at managing the politics of peace and development. Hanoi moved quickly to clap some 100,000 of those prominent in the old regime into "reeducation camps." It followed in the late 1970s by imposing roughshod a program of integrating the south (with its distinct style and strong French and American imprint) into the existing northern system of centralized political control and economic planning. Joblessness, already high because of the large numbers of demobilized soldiers, climbed still higher. A newly collectivized agricultural sector suffered an immediate fall in rice output. The resulting economic crisis together with persecution of ethnic Chinese produced a second round of refugees, the "boat people."

These domestic difficulties were intensified by conflict within the region. Relations with Cambodia deteriorated following border skirmishes provoked by the new Pol Pot regime and climaxing in 1979 with the Vietnamese invasion and occupation of a country gripped by a frenzy of self-destruction. An already suspicious Beijing at once responded by sending a punitive expedition against the upstart Vietnamese. With few friends and with influential Chinese and American enemies, Vietnam became heavily dependent on the Soviet Union both strategically and economically. An annual Soviet subsidy of $1–$2 billion kept a struggling Vietnam afloat through the 1980s.

Hanoi fundamentally revised its course in December 1986 following the death of the dominant figure in the Workers' Party, Le Duan. His replacement, Nguyen Van Linh, was a northerner who had served in the south between 1945 and 1975 and thereafter established a reputation as a maverick reformer. Linh implemented a new economic policy that returned land to peasants, stimulated free markets, encouraged foreign investment, promoted production for export, and tapped the agricultural and commercial expertise of the south. His foreign policy, geared to resolving outstanding conflicts, helped open foreign markets and attract foreign capital, both critical to developing one of the poorest countries in the world. Détente with China followed in 1991 and with the United States in 1995. Returning Americans were astonished by the lack of animosity and bitterness they encountered. Vietnamese had seemingly submerged the trauma of the war in the old and deep tradition of resistance and patriotism. They had played by a familiar national script, and, despite the high price, the promise of victory had been realized.

Cambodia, though it sought to remain a bystander to the conflict in Vietnam, may have suffered even more death and destruction. Incursions by NLF, DRV, Saigon, and American forces, together with devastating and repeated U.S. bombing raids, intensified the havoc already created by civil war and radicalized

Cambodia's own revolutionary forces, the Khmer Rouge. Following Sihanouk's overthrow in 1970, this multifaceted conflict cost the lives of approximately a half million (mostly noncombatants), and roughly half the rural population (more than two million) became refugees, straining the cities and reducing agricultural production. Just as the war in Vietnam died out in April 1975, the Khmer Rouge came to power in what would turn into a reign of terror, starvation, and death. Pol Pot emptied the cities in his quest to purify his country of class enemies, those urbanites tainted by privilege and foreign influence. While some 300,000 of the elite fled into exile, perhaps 20 percent (roughly 1.5 million) of the remaining population died between 1975 and 1979 from revolutionary violence or deprivation. Vietnam's intervention in 1979 toppled the genocidal Khmer Rouge but also set off another cycle of civil conflict. Only in the early 1990s did the turmoil begin to ease.

In comparative terms, it is fair to say that the United States suffered only a flesh wound, although this estimate of the price Americans paid may be particularly difficult to accept for those whose lives were disrupted or whose loved ones were lost in the war. American soldiers killed in action, numbering slightly over 58,000, were but a quarter of the losses suffered by the despised Saigon forces and less than a twentieth of all the Vietnamese lives lost during the U.S. phase of the war. The treasure spent in waging the distant war came to but a small proportion of total national wealth, although a look at the actual numbers can be disconcerting. Military outlays between 1961 and 1975 totaled $141 billion. Long-term obligations such as care for veterans push the figure (by one rough estimate) into the range of $350 billion.

The American wound has been slow to heal, perhaps because the damage was more deeply psychic than physical. Involvement in Vietnam created bitter, deep, and lasting divisions within the country and left painful memories for many who served there (in all, some 2.7 million). So central has Vietnam become as a point of political and cultural reference that it invites comparison to the commanding place of Munich in the mind of an earlier generation. But while Munich and the broader experience of World War II gave rise to the crystalline certainties of the Cold War,

Vietnam has assumed a far more ambiguous status that has made it a source of confusion and contention.

The willed amnesia that set in as the war drew to a close was broken by veterans. They began writing and talking as a form of therapy for what seemed to many troubling, wasted sacrifice. Their personal need to remember and understand forced the Vietnam experience back into the national consciousness. The rediscovery of Vietnam gave rise to acts of homage to those who served, nowhere more dramatically than at the Vietnam Veterans Memorial, built in 1982 in the heart of the capital, hardly a stone's throw from the White House, where the decisions for war had been made. Americans flocked to visit the low, stark black stone slab covered with the names of those who did not return.

The rediscovery of Vietnam also gave rise to disputes over what went wrong and what lessons to draw. Politicians, pundits, and the entertainment industry were soon in full cry. They generally agreed that Vietnam represented a national fall from grace, but differed fundamentally over whether the war was the best and the protest the worst or whether the war itself reflected the worst in the country and the protest the best.

Descendants of the wartime hawks took as their task expunging the blot on U.S. history and character. They placed blame for the first decisive American military defeat and the humiliation of a superpower at the apogee of its strength on Lyndon Johnson's poor leadership, irresponsible guidance by his team of advisers, and a national decline that had eroded patriotism and given rise to a radical antiwar movement. Ronald Reagan's estimate that the Vietnam War was a justified effort to stop the fall of dominoes and "counter the master plan of the communists for world conquest" and that, once America was committed, victory was the only acceptable U.S. goal expressed this influential "revisionist" point of view.[10] The triumphant Grenada and Panama interventions and the Gulf War reflected the determination of Reagan as well as his successor, George Bush, to disprove what many feared Vietnam had shown—that the United States had become a pitiful, helpless giant.

The descendants of the doves traced the origins of Vietnam back to a lamentable Cold War arrogance. The United States had taken upon itself the role of world policeman without knowing the neighborhoods it presumed to patrol and without the informed consent of the American people. The practical conclusion drawn by latter-day doves and shared by much of the public was to approach intervention warily, a viewpoint that put a brake on the foreign-policy activism which was so marked a feature of the Cold War. As a result, Reagan had to reverse course following his intervention in Lebanon, and his involvement in Nicaragua and El Salvador encountered public and congressional opposition so strong that he had to pursue his goals covertly (resulting in the Iran-Contra affair).

The U.S. military drew its own lessons from Vietnam. Commentators took due note of the public impatience with an inconclusive war, the dangers of civilian interference in the conduct of war, and the risks inherent in free media access to the combat zone. The conclusion—applied in Grenada, Panama, and the Persian Gulf—was to fight only where U.S. goals were clear, public support assured, power overwhelming, and thus victory certain. How cautious Vietnam had left the U.S. military became dramatically evident in the Gulf War. The war did yield the quick military victory at a low cost in American lives, as it was designed to do. But it also ended inconclusively, with the agent of aggression, Saddam Hussein, still in power. This outcome did not so much kick as confirm the Vietnam syndrome. Americans nonetheless celebrated the triumph over Iraq as the surrogate for the victory that had eluded them in Vietnam.

Like any dramatic and controversial event, the Vietnam War was soon appropriated by Hollywood and conveyed to a fascinated public as a fantasy world where Americans tested their character, underwent youthful rites of passage, embarked on perilous rescues, suffered personal or national corruption, or replayed frontier dramas with the Vietnamese as the "wild Indians." Seldom in these re-creations did Vietnamese figure as anything more than two-dimensional stock figures. The war remained, as much as during the Cold War, an American drama in which the people of Vietnam played only minor parts.

The crosscurrents at work within the American mind were nowhere more evident than in the issue of normalizing relations with the former tormentor, the Communist leadership still in charge in Hanoi. Standing in the way of normalization were not only families of the missing-in-action but also the gnawing sense of humiliation over the war's outcome and the natural instinct to seek revenge rather than reconciliation. (Hanoi also threw up obstacles, none more troublesome than a 1977 demand for $3 billion in reparations.) But the 1986 changing of the guard in Hanoi led to greater cooperation in accounting for U.S. missing-in-action, thus removing one major obstacle. It also led to the opening of a new market attractive to U.S. corporations. By the early 1990s a majority of Americans supported normalization, and veterans groups were becoming vocal in support of reconciliation. President Bill Clinton, though embarrassed by his own avoidance of service in Vietnam, began the intricate process of rebuilding ties. Accounting for the missing-in-action (down to 1,621 by mid-1995) was the first serious step; removing the travel and trade embargoes was the next; establishing diplomatic relations in 1995 became the last.

The American wound is healing, but a scar remains. The small and distant country of Vietnam is intrinsically hardly more important today than it was when Franklin Roosevelt casually contemplated its future in 1943 or when Truman fatefully placed it within the containment framework in 1950. Vietnam figured, above all else, at each of these and other critical turning points as a test—a test of American character and ideals. How Americans responded was a kind of referendum on their world leadership and the viability of their institutions and values.

But confident Americans with their globe-girdling organization and awesome technology did not prevail. Caught up in their Cold War crusade, U.S. leaders had plunged reluctantly and blindly into Vietnam. What they encountered was a people with a will and solidarity that far exceeded their own, with allies ready to take real risks, and, in the final analysis, with a capacity to absorb the blows of an uneven war undeterred until the enemy—demoralized in the field, divided at home—abandoned Vietnam to its stubborn people, just as the Chinese and the French had done. Americans are likely to continue to examine the war with its unsettling outcome as they might look into a mirror, the better to reflect on not just their recent tumultuous Cold War past but also their long-held claim as a special people.

RECOMMENDED
READING

The Vietnam War is the subject of a wide array of broadly cast accounts (with some especially helpful in giving Vietnamese a prominent place alongside Americans): George C. Herring, *America's Longest War: The United States and Vietnam, 1950–1975* (3rd ed., 1996); William J. Duiker, *U.S. Containment Policy and the Conflict in Indochina* (1994); Marilyn B. Young, *The Vietnam Wars, 1945–1990* (1991); Anthony Short, *The Origins of the Vietnam War* (1989); William S. Turley, *The Second Indochina War: A Short Political and Military History, 1954–1975* (1987); George McT. Kahin, *Intervention: How America Became Involved in Vietnam* (1986); Gabriel Kolko, *Anatomy of a War: Vietnam, the United States and the Modern Historical Experience* (1985); R. B. Smith, *An International History of the Vietnam War* (3 vols., 1983–91), surveying 1955–1966; and the collection edited by Jayne Werner and Luu Doan Huynh, *The Vietnam War: Vietnamese and American Perspectives* (1992). Journalists have served as early and important chroniclers of the war. David Halberstam, *The Best and the Brightest* (1972); Stanley Karnow, *Vietnam: A History* (rev. ed., 1991); and Neil Sheehan, *A Bright Shining Lie: John Paul Vann and America in Vietnam* (1988), stand out for their rich and engaging treatment. Gary R. Hess offers a thoughtful, up-to-date survey of the literature in "The Unending Debate: Historians and the Vietnam War," *Diplomatic History* 18 (Spring 1994).

Appraisals of Kennedy's policy are still sharply divided. John M. Newman, *JFK and Vietnam: Deception, Intrigue, and the Struggle for Power* (1992), makes the case for Kennedy as a reluctant interventionist who finally came to favor disengagement. Stephen Pelz, "John F. Kennedy's 1961 Vietnam War Decisions," *Journal of Strategic Studies* [London] 4 (December 1981), and Lawrence J. Bassett and Stephen E. Pelz, "The Failed Search for Victory: Vietnam and the

Politics of War," in *Kennedy's Quest for Victory: American Foreign Policy, 1961–1963*, ed. Thomas G. Paterson (1989), present the alternative view—Kennedy as a Cold War activist who made a critical commitment. Ellen Hammer, *A Death in November: America in Vietnam, 1963* (1987), and Anne Blair, *Lodge in Vietnam: A Patriot Abroad* (1995), offer fine accounts of the Diem coup and its consequences.

Johnson's decision for war is easily traced thanks to the accessible and revealing holdings of the Lyndon B. Johnson Library (Austin, Texas). Notable studies drawing on those materials include George C. Herring, *LBJ and Vietnam: A Different Kind of War* (1994); David M. Barrett, *Uncertain Warriors: Lyndon Johnson and His Vietnam Advisors* (1993); Brian VanDeMark, *Into the Quagmire: Lyndon Johnson and the Escalation of the Vietnam War* (1991); and Mark Clodfelter, *The Limits of Airpower: The American Bombing of North Vietnam* (1989).

A picture of key figures in the deepening Vietnam commitment emerges from Cecil B. Currey, *Edward Lansdale: The Unquiet American* (1988); Thomas C. Reeves, *A Question of Character: A Life of John F. Kennedy* (1991); Robert S. McNamara, *In Retrospect: The Tragedy and Lessons of Vietnam* (1995); Dean Rusk as told to Richard Rusk, *As I Saw It*, ed. Daniel S. Papp (1990); George W. Ball, *The Past Has Another Pattern* (1982); Paul K. Conkin, *Big Daddy from the Pedernales: Lyndon Baines Johnson* (1986); and Doris Kearns, *Lyndon Johnson and the American Dream* (1976).

The domestic dissension spawned by the Vietnam War is developed by David W. Levy, *The Debate over Vietnam* (1991), a synthesis that contains a helpful guide to the literature; Tom Wells, *The War Within: America's Battle over Vietnam* (1994); Charles DeBenedetti assisted by Charles Chatfield, *An American Ordeal: The Antiwar Movement of the Vietnam Era* (1990); Melvin Small, *Johnson, Nixon, and the Doves* (1988); Daniel C. Hallin, *The "Uncensored War": The Media and Vietnam* (1986); Kathleen J. Turner, *Lyndon Johnson's Dual War: Vietnam and the Press* (1985); and John E. Mueller, *War, Presidents and Public Opinion* (1973).

For broad attempts to make sense of the U.S. misadventure in Vietnam in terms of patterns in American society and culture, see Loren Baritz, *Backfire: A History of How American Culture Led Us into Vietnam and Made Us Fight the Way We Did* (1985); James W. Gibson, *The Perfect War: The War We Couldn't Lose and How We Did* (1988); Susan Jeffords, *The Remasculinization of America: Gender and the Vietnam War* (1989); and John Hellman, *American Myth and the Legacy of Vietnam* (1986).

The general Vietnamese perspective on the war emerges from William J. Duiker, *Sacred War: Nationalism and Revolution in a Divided Vietnam* (1995), with its helpful survey of the literature, and Frances FitzGerald, *Fire in the Lake: The Vietnamese and the Americans in Vietnam* (1972), a pioneering and prize-winning attempt by a nonspecialist to give life to the "other side." Such key topics as Vietnamese nationalism and the appeal of communist doctrine are treated in Keith W. Taylor, *The Birth of Vietnam* (1983); Truong Buu Lam, ed. and trans., *Patterns of Vietnamese Response to Foreign Intervention, 1858–1900* (1967); Alexander Woodside, *Community and Revolution in Modern Vietnam* (1976); Hue-Tam Ho Tai, *Radicalism and the Origins of the Vietnamese Revolution* (1992); David G. Marr, *Vietnamese Tradition on Trial, 1920–1945* (1981); and Huynh Kim Khanh, *Vietnamese Communism, 1925–1945* (1982). The best account of Ho's life is Jean Lacouture, *Ho Chi Minh: A Political Biography*, trans. Peter Wiles (1968).

For the southern opposition to Diem and the United States, see Truong Nhu Tang with David Chanoff and Doan Van Toai, *A Viet Cong Memoir* (1985), and Carlyle A. Thayer, *War by Other Means: National Liberation and Revolution in Viet-Nam, 1954–60* (1989). Three regional studies are critical to understanding rural politics and rural conflict during the period of deepening American involvement: Jeffrey Race, *War Comes to Long An: Revolutionary Conflict in a Vietnamese Province* (1972); James W. Trullinger, Jr., *Village at War: An Account of Revolution in Vietnam* (1980); and Eric M. Bergerud, *The Dynamics of Defeat: The Vietnam War in Hau Nghia Province* (1991).

NOTES

CHAPTER 1

1. William J. Lederer and Eugene Burdick, *The Ugly American* (New York: Norton, 1958), 267, 285.
2. Roosevelt phrase from conversation of 15 March 1945, in U.S. Department of State, *Foreign Relations of the United States* [hereafter *FRUS*], *1945*, vol. 1 (Washington: Government Printing Office, 1967), 124.
3. Quotes from reports by consul general in Saigon Charles S. Reed II and vice-consul in Hanoi James O'Sullivan, in *FRUS, 1947*, vol. 6 (Washington: Government Printing Office, 1972), 114, 120, 124.
4. *FRUS, 1948*, vol. 6 (Washington: Government Printing Office, 1974), 28.
5. Acheson statement of 1 February 1950, in *Department of State Bulletin* 22 (13 February 1950): 244.
6. Quotes from National Security Council top-secret policy statement no. 64 of 27 February 1950 (approved by Truman on 24 April 1950), and no. 124/2 of 25 June 1952 (approved by Truman that same day), in *FRUS, 1950*, vol. 6 (Washington: Government Printing Office, 1976), 745, and in *FRUS, 1952–1954*, vol. 12 (Washington: Government Printing Office, 1984), 128.
7. Truman message to Congress, 24 May 1951, in *Public Papers of the Presidents: Harry S. Truman, 1951* (Washington: Government Printing Office, 1965), 309.
8. Quotes from Eisenhower's address at Gettysburg College, 4 April 1959, in *Public Papers of the Presidents: Dwight D. Eisenhower, 1959* (Washington: Government Printing Office, 1960), 311; from his letter to Churchill, 4 April 1954, in *FRUS, 1952–1954*, vol. 13, pt. 1 (Washington: Government Printing Office, 1982),

1240; and from his press conference of 7 April 1954, in *Public Papers of the Presidents: Dwight D. Eisenhower, 1954* (Washington: Government Printing Office, 1960), 383.

CHAPTER 2

1. Vera Vladimirovna Vishnyakova-Akimova, *Two Years in Revolutionary China, 1925–1927*, trans. Steven I. Levine (Cambridge: Harvard East Asian Research Center, 1971), 229.
2. Quoted in *Patterns of Vietnamese Response to Foreign Intervention, 1858–1900*, ed. and trans. Truong Buu Lam (New Haven, Conn.: Yale Southeast Asia Studies, 1967), 107.
3. Ho Chi Minh's April 1960 recollections in Ho, *Selected Writings (1920–1969)* (Hanoi: Foreign Languages Publishing House, 1973), 250.
4. Ho, *Selected Writings*, 251.
5. Ho, *Selected Writings*, 45–46.
6. Jean Lacouture, *Ho Chi Minh: A Political Biography*, trans. Peter Wiles (New York: Random House, 1968), 81–82.
7. Truong Buu Lam, *Patterns of Vietnamese Response*, 8.
8. Quotes from Keith W. Taylor, *The Birth of Vietnam* (Berkeley: University of California Press, 1983), 301, and Nguyen Kim Khanh, *Vietnamese Communism, 1925–1945* (Ithaca: Cornell University Press, 1982), 29–30n.
9. Statement of 2 September 1945, in Ho, *Selected Writings*, 56.
10. Ho's political report of February 1951, in Ho, *Selected Writings*, 123.
11. Quoted in Chen Jian, "China and the First Indo-China War, 1950–54," *China Quarterly*, no. 133 (March 1993): 92.
12. From a set of interviews collected by Gérard Chaliand in October-November 1967 and published in his *The Peasants of North Vietnam*, trans. Peter Wiles (Baltimore: Penguin, 1969), 143.
13. Ho, *Selected Writings*, 177.
14. Comment by Le Van Chan (a pseudonym), a party member who had served in the upper echelon of the southern branch of the party organization before his capture in 1962, in Jeffrey Race, *War Comes to Long An: Revolutionary Conflict in a Vietnamese Province* (Berkeley: University of California Press, 1972), 97.
15. Race, *War Comes to Long An*, 98.
16. Quote from Neil Sheehan, *A Bright Shining Lie: John Paul Vann and America in Vietnam* (New York: Random House, 1988), 265. *Bright Shining Lie*, 203–65, offers a detailed account of Ap Bac,

which Sheehan revisits in his *After the War Was Over: Hanoi and Saigon* (New York: Random House, 1992), 123–29.

17. From the record of the 17 March 1960 National Security Council meeting, in U.S. Department of State, *Foreign Relations of the United States, 1958–1960*, vol. 6 (Washington: Government Printing Office, 1991), 857, 858.

CHAPTER 3

1. Quoted in Merrill D. Peterson, *Adams and Jefferson: A Revolutionary Dialogue* (Athens: University of Georgia Press, 1976), 81.
2. David Halberstam, *The Best and the Brightest* (New York: Random House, 1972), 41.
3. Henry F. Graff, *The Tuesday Cabinet: Deliberation and Decision on Peace and War under Lyndon B. Johnson* (Englewood Cliffs, N.J.: Prentice-Hall, 1970), 48.
4. Halberstam, *Best and Brightest*, 41.
5. Thomas C. Reeves, *A Question of Character: A Life of John F. Kennedy* (New York: Norton, 1991), 46.
6. Kennedy quotes from his introductory comments dated 1 January 1960, in *The Strategy of Peace*, ed. Allen Nevins (New York: Harper, 1960), 6, 8; and *Public Papers of the Presidents: John F. Kennedy* [hereafter *PPP: JFK*], *1961* (Washington: Government Printing Office, 1962), 1.
7. Quotes from Richard D. Mahoney, *JFK: Ordeal in Africa* (New York: Oxford University Press, 1983), 14; and Kennedy, *Strategy*, 64.
8. U.S. Department of State, *Foreign Relations of the United States* [hereafter *FRUS*], *1961–1963*, vol. 1 (Washington: Government Printing Office, 1988), 12; U.S. Department of Defense, *United States–Vietnam Relations, 1945–1967* (12 books; Washington: Government Printing Office, 1971), bk. 11, 3.
9. *FRUS, 1961–1963*, 1: 72.
10. Quotes from *FRUS, 1961–1963*, 1: 74, 131.
11. *Department of State Bulletin* 45 (7 August 1961): 234–37.
12. *The Pentagon Papers: The Defense Department History of United States Decisionmaking on Vietnam* [Senator Gravel ed.] (5 vols.; Boston: Beacon Press, 1971–72), 2: 653, 654.
13. *FRUS, 1961–1963*, 1: 382, 575.
14. *FRUS, 1961–1963*, 1: 605.
15. U.S. Department of Defense, *United States–Vietnam Relations, 1945–1967*, bk. 11, 360–61.
16. Quotes from *FRUS, 1961–1963*, 1: 532, 577; and Arthur M.

Schlesinger, Jr., A *Thousand Days: John F. Kennedy in the White House* (Boston: Houghton Mifflin, 1965), 547.

17. Quotes from *FRUS, 1961–1963*, 1: 643, 677, 705; letter to Diem in *PPP: JFK, 1961,* 801; and Benjamin C. Bradlee, *Conversations with Kennedy* (New York: Norton, 1975), 58.
18. JFK quoted in Townsend Hoopes, *The Limits of Intervention* (rev. ed.; New York: Norton, 1987), 21.
19. McNamara quoted in Henry L. Trewhitt, *McNamara* (New York: Harper and Row, 1971), 201; Rusk address of 22 April 1963, in *Pentagon Papers,* 2: 821.
20. Quotes from *FRUS, 1961–1963,* vol. 3 (Washington: Government Printing Office, 1991), 628; *FRUS, 1961–1963,* vol. 4 (Washington: Government Printing Office, 1991), 21.
21. *FRUS, 1961–1963,* 4: 93–94.
22. Quotes from *FRUS, 1961–1963,* 4: 252, 379, 393.
23. *FRUS, 1961–1963,* 1: 468.
24. *FRUS, 1961–1963,* vol. 2 (Washington: Government Printing Office, 1990), 297.
25. *PPP: JFK, 1963* (Washington: Government Printing Office, 1964), 569.

CHAPTER 4

1. LBJ quoted in Doris Kearns, *Lyndon Johnson and the American Dream* (New York: Harper and Row, 1976), 251–52.
2. LBJ speech in the House of Representatives, 7 May 1947, quoted in Brian VanDeMark, *Into the Quagmire: Lyndon Johnson and the Escalation of the Vietnam War* (New York: Oxford University Press, 1991), 9.
3. Quote from Paul K. Conkin, *Big Daddy from the Pedernales: Lyndon Baines Johnson* (Boston: Twayne, 1986), 168.
4. LBJ quoted in George C. Herring and Richard H. Immerman, "Eisenhower, Dulles, and Dienbienphu: 'The Day We Didn't Go to War' Revisited," *Journal of American History* 71 (September 1984): 353; and *The Pentagon Papers: The Defense Department History of United States Decisionmaking on Vietnam* [Senator Gravel ed.] (5 vols.; Boston: Beacon Press, 1971–72), 2: 58.
5. Quotes from U.S. Department of State, *Foreign Relations of the United States* [hereafter *FRUS*], *1961–1963,* vol. 1 (Washington: Government Printing Office, 1988): 150, 154; and *Pentagon Papers,* 2: 57–58.
6. LBJ comments from 31 August meeting, in *FRUS, 1961–1963,* vol. 4 (Washington: Government Printing Office, 1991): 74.

7. LBJ quoted in *FRUS, 1961–1963,* 4: 636, and in Bill Moyers, "Flashbacks," *Newsweek* 85 (10 February 1975): 76.

8. Quotes from *FRUS, 1961–1963,* 4: 636–38.

9. McNamara in *FRUS, 1961–1963,* 4: 732, 735.

10. *FRUS, 1961–1963,* 4: 745–47.

11. Quotes from *FRUS, 1964–1968,* vol. 1 (Washington: Government Printing Office, 1992): 15–16; *Pentagon Papers,* 3: 498.

12. Quote from Henry L. Trewhitt, *McNamara* (New York: Harper and Row, 1971), 257.

13. LBJ's phrase quoted from Robert S. McNamara with Brian VanDeMark, *In Retrospect: The Tragedy and Lessons of Vietnam* (New York: Times Books, 1995), 112.

14. *FRUS, 1964–1968,* 1: 157–58.

15. *Public Papers of the Presidents: Lyndon B. Johnson* [hereafter *PPP: LBJ*], *1963–64* (2 vols.; Washington: Government Printing Office, 1965), 1: 370.

16. From speeches of 12 August and 21 October 1964, both in *PPP: LBJ, 1963–64,* 2: 953 and 1391.

17. Quotes from *Pentagon Papers,* 3: 718, 722; and David Halberstam, *The Best and the Brightest* (New York: Random House, 1972), 414.

18. Meiczyslaw Maneli, *War of the Vanquished,* trans. Maria de Görgey (New York: Harper and Row, 1971), 154.

19. Central Committee of the Workers' Party, secret resolution of December 1963, in *Vietnam: A History in Documents,* ed. Gareth Porter (New York: New American Library, 1981), 256–57.

20. Gareth Porter, "Coercive Diplomacy in Vietnam: The Tonkin Gulf Crisis Reconsidered," in *The American War in Vietnam,* ed. Jayne Werner and David Hunt (Ithaca: Cornell Southeast Asia Program, 1993), 9–22.

21. Chen Jian, "China's Involvement with the Vietnam War, 1964–69," *China Quarterly,* no. 142 (June 1995): 356–87.

22. Le Duan, speech to a cadre conference, 6–8 July 1965, in *Vietnam: The Definitive Documentation of Human Decisions,* ed. Gareth Porter (2 vols.; Stanfordville, N.Y.: Earl M. Coleman Enterprises, 1979), 2: 383–85.

23. Taylor report to Washington in late November, in *FRUS, 1964–1968,* 1: 948, 950, 954.

24. Bundy to Johnson, 27 January and 7 February 1965, in tabs 10 and 22, National Security Council History, Deployment of Major U.S. Forces to Vietnam, July 1965, National Security File, Lyndon Baines Johnson Library, Austin, Texas [hereafter Vietnam Deployment].

25. Quotes from *Pentagon Papers*, 3: 354; Eric F. Goldman, *The Tragedy of Lyndon Johnson* (New York: Knopf, 1969), 404; and Lyndon Baines Johnson, *The Vantage Point: Perspectives of the Presidency, 1963–1969* (New York: Holt, Rinehart and Winston, 1971), 125.

26. LBJ to Ambassador Taylor, 30 December 1964 and 27 January 1965, in *FRUS, 1964–1968*, 1: 1059, and in tab 13, Vietnam Deployment.

27. *PPP: LBJ, 1965* (2 vols.; Washington: Government Printing Office, 1966), 1: 394–99 (italics in the original).

28. Ball's memo, reproduced in *Atlantic Monthly* 230 (July 1972): 49.

29. VanDeMark, *Into the Quagmire*, 140.

30. Henry F. Graff, *The Tuesday Cabinet: Deliberation and Decision on Peace and War under Lyndon B. Johnson* (Englewood Cliffs, N.J.: Prentice-Hall, 1970), 54.

31. Rostow memo of 20 May 1965, in *Pentagon Papers*, 3: 382.

32. Quote from Bundy memo of 30 June 1965, in tab 354, Vietnam Deployment.

33. Quote from Rusk memo, 23 February 1965, used in talk with LBJ, in tab 82, Vietnam Deployment; Rusk address before the American Society of International Law, 23 April 1965, in *Pentagon Papers*, 3: 733–36.

34. McNamara off-the-record remarks to Arthur Krock, 22 April 1965, in *America in Vietnam: A Documentary History*, ed. William Appleman Williams et al. (Garden City, N.Y.: Doubleday, 1985), 247–48.

35. *PPP: LBJ, 1965*, 2: 794–803.

36. Quotes from McGeorge Bundy to LBJ, 9 February and 30 June 1965, in tabs 32 and 354, Vietnam Deployment; and McNamara, *In Retrospect*, 190.

37. Quotes from Mansfield to LBJ, 6 January and 9 December 1964, in *FRUS, 1964–1968*, 1: 2–3, and in box 12, folder CO 312, Confidential File, Johnson Papers.

38. Humphrey to LBJ, 15 February 1965, reproduced in Hubert Humphrey, *The Education of a Public Man: My Life and Politics* (Garden City, N.Y.: Doubleday, 1976), 322–23; Clifford to LBJ, 17 May, tab 223, Vietnam Deployment; Clifford prediction of 25 July 1965, and Mansfield comment in LBJ meeting with congressional leaders, 27 July 1965, both in box 1, Meeting Notes File, Johnson Papers.

39. Quotes from George W. Ball, *The Past Has Another Pattern* (New

York: Norton, 1982), 383, and Ball to LBJ, 1 July 1965, in *Pentagon Papers*, 4: 616.
40. Box 1, Meeting Notes File, Johnson Papers.
41. Halberstam, *Best and Brightest*, 512, 564.

CHAPTER 5

1. McNamara to LBJ, 30 November 1965, in *The Pentagon Papers: The Defense Department History of United States Decisionmaking on Vietnam* [Senator Gravel ed.] (5 vols.; Boston: Beacon Press, 1971–72), 4: 623.
2. Quotes from meetings of 17 and 18 December, in box 1, Meeting Notes File, Johnson Papers, Lyndon Baines Johnson Library, Austin, Texas.
3. Philip Caputo, *A Rumor of War* (New York: Ballantine, 1978), 234.
4. Truong Nhu Tang with David Chanoff and Doan Van Toai, *A Viet Cong Memoir* (New York: Random House, 1985), 168.
5. Doris Kearns, *Lyndon Johnson and the American Dream* (New York: Harper and Row, 1976), 283.
6. Quotes from Kearns, *Lyndon Johnson*, 313; Tom Wells, *The War Within: America's Battle over Vietnam* (Berkeley: University of California Press, 1994), 69; and Henry F. Graff, *The Tuesday Cabinet: Deliberation and Decision on Peace and War under Lyndon B. Johnson* (Englewood Cliffs, N.J.: Prentice-Hall, 1970), 100.
7. Nixon speeches of 14 May 1969, in *Public Papers of the Presidents: Richard Nixon, 1969* (Washington: Government Printing Office, 1971), 370; and 30 April 1970, in *Public Papers of the Presidents: Richard Nixon, 1970* (Washington: Government Printing Office, 1971), 409.
8. Huong Van Ba quoted in David Chanoff and Doan Van Toai, *Portrait of the Enemy* (New York: Random House, 1986), 155.
9. Quoted in Tiziano Terzani, *Giai Phong! The Fall and Liberation of Saigon*, trans. John Shepley (New York: Ballantine, 1977), 105.
10. Charles D. Hobbs, *Ronald Reagan's Call to Action* (Nashville, Tenn.: Thomas Nelson, 1976), 42.

INDEX

Acheson, Dean, 10, 46, 48
Adams, John, 42, 43
Ali, Muhammad, 112
antiwar movement, *see* peace
   movement
Ap Bac, battle of, 37–40, 62, 63
Army, U.S., 56; Special Warfare
   School, 57
Associated Press, 62
Australia, 108; in SEATO, 13

Baez, Joan, 112
Ball, George, 63, 64, 94, 96,
   103
Bao Dai, 10, 14, 29, 32
Bay of Pigs invasion, 56, 57
Berlin, 52, 56
Best and the Brightest, The (Halber-
   stam), 42
boat people, 124
Bolsheviks, 21, 26
Britain, 108–9; and Geneva agree-
   ments, 12, 13; and Malaya, 36; in
   SEATO, 13; in World War II, 5–
   7
Browne, Malcolm, 62
Buddhists, 63–65, 85, 89
Bundy, McGeorge, 47–49, 58, 65,
   90–93, 96, 101, 115–16

Burdick, Eugene, 3–5
Bush, George, 126

California, University of, at Berkeley, 44
Cambodia, 11, 30, 86, 125; as
   French colony, 5; gains independence, 13; U.S. bombing of,
   119, 122; Vietnamese occupation
   of, 124
Canada, 108
Castro, Fidel, 56
Catholics, 13–15, 52, 66, 89
Central Intelligence Agency (CIA),
   41, 79, 95, 96; Lansdale and, 15–
   16; in Laos, 55, 57; peace movement and, 114, 119; in Vietnam,
   64, 65, 108
Chiang Kai-shek, 6
China, 18, 70, 87, 88, 93, 97, 106,
   112; and bombing of North Vietnam, 91; Communist victory in,
   10, 31, 46, 79; détente with, 124;
   historical relationship between
   Vietnam and, 24, 128; Nationalist, 21, 30; Nixon and, 118; risk
   of war with, 96, 104; and Tonkin
   Gulf incident, 90; in World
   War II, 5, 6, 22